FACING RACE

FACING RACE

The Gospel in an Ignatian Key

Roger Haight, SJ

ORBIS BOOKS
Maryknoll, New York 10545

Founded in 1970, Orbis Books endeavors to publish works that enlighten the mind, nourish the spirit, and challenge the conscience. The publishing arm of the Maryknoll Fathers and Brothers, Orbis seeks to explore the global dimensions of the Christian faith and mission, to invite dialogue with diverse cultures and religious traditions, and to serve the cause of reconciliation and peace. The books published reflect the views of their authors and do not represent the official position of the Maryknoll Society. To learn more about Maryknoll and Orbis Books, please visit our website at www.orbisbooks.com.

Library of Congress Cataloging-in-Publication Data

Names: Haight, Roger, author.
Title: Facing race : the gospel in an Ignatian key / Roger Haight, S.J.
Description: Maryknoll, NY : Orbis Books, [2024] | Includes bibliographical references and index. | Summary: "A reading of the Ignatian Spiritual Exercises in which the social reality of racism provides a concrete reference for the meaning of sin" — Provided by publisher.
Identifiers: LCCN 2024017100 (print) | LCCN 2024017101 (ebook) | ISBN 9781626985858 (trade paperback) | ISBN 9798888660409 (epub)
Subjects: LCSH: Race relations—Religious aspects—Christianity. | Racism—Religious aspects—Christianity. | Social justice—Religious aspects—Christianity. | Ignatius, of Loyola, Saint, 1491-1556. Exercitia spiritualia.
Classification: LCC BT734.2 .H25 2024 (print) | LCC BT734.2 (ebook) | DDC 241/.675—dc23/eng/20240523
LC record available at https://lccn.loc.gov/2024017100
LC ebook record available at https://lccn.loc.gov/2024017101

Contents

Preface

Some years ago, Pamela Cooper White, Union Theological Seminary's academic dean, asked me to teach a course that discussed how Christian spirituality as a practice and discipline might support the lives of people who work against the many forms of social injustice that infect our lives today. Because I am a Jesuit, I naturally turned to the Spiritual Exercises of Ignatius of Loyola as a way of formulating the dynamics of Christian spirituality. Among the forms of social injustice found in the United States, racism stands out. The analysis contained in this work grew out of the application of the Exercises to racism in America and expanded beyond the limitations of the course on both sides of the interaction.

On the side of what is called "race," I became familiar with Black culture in a parish community on the South Side of Chicago when I was a graduate student and later when I taught for seven years in an integrated neighborhood. Living and working in Asia for many years taught me to appreciate another culture's dynamics, surely not "from inside," but closely enough to appreciate another ethos as different, autonomous, coherent, and valuable. Living within another culture involves constant learning, even without formal analysis, and one of the deepest lessons learned falls within the domain of self-knowledge: one cannot really speak for a culture not one's own. In this work I give Blacks their own voice.

On the side of "spirituality," I expected to find a body of literature that factored racism into the sphere of Ignatian spirituality but found little that fitted my needs. Analytical appreciation of the Exercises has not caught up to a critical appreciation of racism. A growing body of practical resources for administering the Exercises in a way that directly shapes meditations has begun to appear, but the analytical work of adapting the Exercises to a racially unjust social and cultural framework is only beginning. This allows me to state clearly at the outset that I do not appeal to the Spiritual Exercises of Ignatius as a studied expositor. Rather, as a theologian, I look to the text of Ignatius as mirroring the narrative structure of the formation of Christian faith as a distinctive spiritual tradition. By penetrating to the nature of Christian faith, the Exercises are able to show clearly that one cannot be a Christian racist, that Christian faith is intrinsically anti-racist.[1]

This work offers a theological analysis of Christian spirituality in the face of racism in America. It looks at existential spirituality as the way persons or groups lead their lives in relation to what they consider ultimate. The significant element of this open view lies in ultimacy, the supreme value operative in a person's life. This centering value pro-

---

1. The obvious retort to this assertion says it cannot be true because there are so many Christian racists. This is no slight observation. But I hope to reply to it through theology as a normative discipline rather than by moral exhortation. My conclusion is either that Christian racists are not really Christian or that many of us are Christians in an ignorant, or incoherent, or self-willed, or deficient way.

vides the formal criterion for gathering all the things that human beings consciously do within the sphere of spirituality, making it an intimate mantle that wraps identity with comprehensive meaning. Spirituality so understood means that all people have some spirituality. The comprehensive understanding of spirituality shows the importance it carries for a given person or group. The following pages put spirituality at the center of Christianity and show how it should position the churches relative to racism in American culture and society.

Something about spirituality tends to restrict it to an individualistic and private sphere, at least in the United States. This does not necessarily entail a lack of social consciousness on the part of one who attends to a spiritual life. But human beings possess an ability to construct compartments in life that are distinct from others. Such a process helps impose order on the world and within one's own life. Yet it often results in restricting spirituality to a domain so solitary that its intrinsic social dimensions remain hidden from the self.[2]

It may be taken for granted today that in a land of religious plurality each person is free to define their own religious identity. The American Constitution seeks to preserve religion and thus spiritual freedom from outside interference and to protect government from religious particularism. While this may not be entirely successful, at least it has allowed religious pluralism to thrive in America. But the result of this protection also leans toward privatization of one's personal spirituality, even within a given

---

2. "Racial oppression requires and stimulates in the oppressors a lack of recognition of the full humanity of the exploited and racialized others." Joe R. Faegin, *Systematic Racism: A Theory of Oppression* (New York: Routledge, 2006), 27.

religious tradition. In the end, despite all the external influences, I alone am responsible for my spiritual relationship with God.

Another line of reflection runs counter to individualism and the privatization of spirituality. It draws evidence from personal self-consciousness, developmental psychology, and the very structure of religious consciousness. Innumerable factors feed into everyone's social subjectivity. People cannot realistically imagine themselves apart from the world to which they belong. A newborn requires a long period of care and input to develop an integrated personality. Individual persons cannot come to any self-definition without considering the narrative of the many influences that have helped shape them. Pierre Teilhard de Chardin offered a striking image for the social constitution of the self: We exist supported by the two hands of God. One creating hand of God directly holds us in existence; the other co-creating hand of God, itself created by God, is the world of nature, society, and those individual beings that nurture us along the way.[3] People are social individuals whether they know it or not. Our conscience and our deepest spiritualities are ours and at the same time continually given to us.

This book is about Christian spirituality. It proposes a theological account of the inner dynamics of Christian life. The tensive relationship between being a member of the Christian community and being an autonomous individual citizen runs through the pages of this work. Theology appeals to the community's authoritative sources, but actual Christian behavior is driven by more social and particular reasons than can be told. The response of the citizen fre-

---

3. Pierre Teilhard de Chardin, *The Divine Milieu: An Essay on the Interior Life* (New York: Harper & Brothers, 1960), 47–51.

quently contradicts the spirituality of the community. The conjunction of the two perspectives, the distinguishing and the holding together, complicates the task of explaining why Christian spirituality has to overcome individualism and privatization in order to become accountable to or for structural social issues generally, and in this case racism.

I have chosen to use the Spiritual Exercises of Ignatius Loyola as a tool for analyzing this task partly because it represents my own religious family.[4] But Ignatius's Exercises are more than idiosyncratically his own; they reflect the initial genesis of Christianity and give expression to the essence of its spirituality. The reasons for this were mainly accidents of history. The catalyst of Ignatius's conversion from military and political operative to Christian pilgrim was occasioned by a wound in battle and the reading material available to him in convalescence. He had the gospel texts contained within a larger compendium of commentary. He became so focused on Jesus that he transcribed his words as they appeared in the gospel stories. He thus assumed a new persona by a fixation on Jesus and an intense internalization of the desire to become a disciple. His rebirth reenacted the pattern that generated the gospels, and this, in turn, is reflected in his Spiritual Exercises.

But the dramatic story of Ignatius's conversion also reinforces its appeal to individual persons. Although he sought to share with others his experiences of taking up a new way of life, he offered the Spiritual Exercises to individuals rather than to societies or for the cure of social disease. Even as a tool of Jesuit formation, they appeal to each one as part of a process of socialization. They deal almost exclusively

---

4. Ignatius Loyola, *The Spiritual Exercises of Saint Ignatius*, ed. George E. Ganss (Chicago: Loyola Press, 1992).

with personal sin and its mythic background as found in scripture and doctrine, and they offer each individual who makes them a path of personal life that focuses particular attention on each one's past, present, and future. The Exercises were not composed in order to call attention and respond to structural social sin but to individual sin in order to release personal freedom and commitment.

The language of personal sin as distinct from structural sin sets up the deeper problem that this book addresses. Personal sin, although occasioned by history and circumstance, always wells up from within subjectivity and freedom, so that each one is accountable for it. Sin refers to moral defection from a norm; it is something for which a person is responsible and guilty. Structural sin, by contrast, refers to patterns of behavior in a social body that exist prior to any given individual who enters and participates in the group. Relative to each individual member, structural sin is part of the world as he or she finds it. Young people do not share individual responsibility for patterns into which they are socialized.[5] The idea of structural sin as distinct from evil thus seems inherently paradoxical. If this be the case, the Ignatian language that calls for shame and repentance for personal sinful acts does not fit an often-unknowing participation in structural sin, patterns of behavior that may contribute to the ruin of many innocent victims even though the actions seem normal and are legally protected.

On this supposition, using the structure of the Spiritual Exercises as a program that addresses the structural sins of society rather than the personal sins of individuals requires

---

5. These are typological descriptions rather than close analytical concepts: one can imagine someone designing a structurally sinful organized crime and another person innocent of his or her materially sinful behavior.

an adjustment of language. Refocusing the Spiritual Exercises on participation in a culture and society that one calls sinful and thus involves moral guilt also shifts the goal of the Exercises. This is not an easy process, and it requires distinctions and appropriate language for its applicability. For example, when Ignacio Ellacuría was leading the Spiritual Exercises for Jesuits in San Salvador in the late 1960s and early 1970s, his fundamental intention was less to renew their personal lives as each one had done for years, and more to make them aware of the sinful dimensions of the social and cultural context in which they were living.[6] This required less an examination of conscience and more an examination of the social reality of systemic poverty and conflict in which they lived. Like all the light we cannot see before we turn a new telescope on the vast space above, so too an examination of our own societies uncovers the systemic repression, physical and mental suffering, and restriction of opportunity and creativity of Blacks that remain hidden in a routine status quo. Social analysis examines the relations that we do not see or to which we've become accustomed: the perceptions, the ideas, the values, the feelings, the joys, the psychic energy, the fears, the stifled freedom, the dead ends, the impasses, the ordinary goals that remain impossible for so many, all the things present in society that remain invisible or taken for granted without examination.

This work aims at directing the Christian imagination toward the sin of racism through the lens of the gospel mediated by the Ignatian Spiritual Exercises. It views racism not as personal sin but as structural sin, a notion that is real but

_____

6. I will expand this example in Chapter III. The point here is to underline the character of this work as trying to capture the intrinsic logic of Christian spirituality in the face of fundamental flaws in American culture and society.

subtle and requires explanation. Its purpose is not to uncover particular acts of racism, but to expand people's consciousness and conscience. It seeks to open up and reveal a still largely hidden world that contains a moral imperative for a common good. This social interpretation does not substitute for or compete with a traditional use of the Exercises. It is directed to those who are interested in the dynamics of racism, Christian spirituality, the Spiritual Exercises of Ignatius Loyola, and theology as a discipline. For spirituality is not only continually informed by theology but may also open new horizons that elicit new theological understanding that in turn transforms a Christian way of life.

This is a work of Christian theology. The discussion begins with a brief theoretical statement about the nature of the discipline and the role played by the Spiritual Exercises.[7] Two main reasons account for this formal introduction. The first comes from its implied audience that includes but also reaches beyond the Christian faith community. One could write this book with an extended exegesis of Jesus's parable of the Good Samaritan. But in an intercommunicating religiously plural world, Christian theologians have to appeal to more extensive foundations than the authority of a tradition's sources. Christian theology must explicitly aim at a language that appeals to commonly accepted humanistic ideas and values. This book makes the case that Christian faith intrinsically rejects racism and that this stance will find

---

7. Those unconcerned with discussions of method may begin reading with Chapter II. Those completely unfamiliar with the discipline of theology may be frustrated with the abstract character of this initial discussion. And those familiar with such things may be unconvinced of a need for it. Nevertheless, as a prelude, it defines the theological viewpoint operative in this work.

resonance with other faith traditions with whom we may create common cause.

The other reason relates to the use of the Spiritual Exercises of Ignatius Loyola, which occupies a particular place among many Christian schools of spirituality. As such, it carries a substantial tradition of literature about its history and contemporary practice. But the theological appeal to the Exercises in this work narrows the focus of attention to basic issues. One is found in an appeal to a particular interpretation of the elementary structure of the Spiritual Exercises: its initial focus on sin, its turn to the ministry of Jesus, and its purpose of drawing forth from a person a commitment to a form of action. Another rests in a correlation of that basic structure with the way persons are drawn to Christian faith itself. These moves do not add up to a desire to dictate how the Exercises should be adapted to specific Christian seekers. But it supports the affirmation of the Catholic bishops in Synod in 1971: "Action on behalf of justice and participation in the transformation of the world fully appear to us as a constitutive dimension of the preaching of the gospel."[8] The initial discussion of theology forms the basis of this claim by grounding Christian anti-racism in the very structure and essence of Christian faith. The world demands a deep account of the hope that is within us (1 Pet 3:15).

An overview of the chapters will set the direction of the discussion. The first chapter presents a number of basic ideas underlying the Christian theology that informs the presentation. The plurality of religious traditions in America and the pluralism of Christian theologies require that certain

---

8. Synod of Bishops, "Justice in the World" (Nov. 30, 1971), #6.

traditional ideas be revised lest the project be compromised.[9] This analysis draws Christian theology and the Spiritual Exercises into a distinctive situation of social injustice. And both are being reinterpreted because the situation calls upon them to formulate a Christian self-understanding and way of life that address society. Theology probes the way Christian spirituality is applied to the context, and spirituality challenges theology to show the relevance of Christian faith for how to react to a racist society. Theology and spirituality unite in following the Exercises back to Jesus and his Hebrew ancestors for a religious response to racism.

The second chapter describes racism directed against African Americans. This limitation of the range of racism does not reflect the depth, complexity, and expansiveness of the phenomenon in American life. Racism draws into itself other sources, biases, resentments, and forms of aggressiveness that mark American history and present-day life, such as Eurocentrism and a colonialist imagination. Rather than offer an archaeology of racism, the imaginative framework of this work focuses on the case of African Americans. Such a chapter should be excerpted from James Baldwin or Ta-Nehisi Coates. But the chapters that follow the description of racism require the author's understanding of the subject

---

9. These adjustments are in line with the "paradigm shift" that Pope Francis calls for in his *motu proprio* "Ad Theologiam Promovendam" (Nov. 1, 2023). He writes: "It is a matter of the pastoral 'stamp' that theology as a whole, and not only in one of its particular spheres, must assume: without opposing theory and practice, theological reflection is urged to develop with an inductive method, which starts from the different contexts and concrete situations in which peoples are inserted, allowing itself to be seriously challenged by reality, in order to become discernment of the 'signs of the times' in the proclamation of the salvific event of the God-agape, communicated in Jesus Christ" (#8).

matter. The brevity and objectivity of the account may require indulgence from those more deeply affected by the injury of racism.

The third, fourth, and fifth chapters of the book correlate with a three-part understanding of the structure of the Spiritual Exercises. They may briefly be characterized as (a) a consciousness of sin, in this case the structural sin of racism that infects American society, (b) a turn to Jesus of Nazareth as found in the gospels and what he represented by his ministry, and (c) an appropriation of Jesus into the lives of people who make the Exercises, with racism as the sin that must be addressed. This basic structure corresponds with the way many theologians across the centuries have represented as a common structure of both revelation and a personal conversion to Christian faith. The dynamic structure of the Exercises captures something foundational in the logic of Christian life.

This three-dimensional structure also uncannily resembles what Edward Schillebeeckx called a negative experience of contrast. He believed that the starting point for ethics lies not in an awareness of an ordered world that is rationally coherent, but of the actual world where things are disordered. Moral reasoning begins with a deep experience of unease and then indignation at the evil in a situation that should not be. The same outrage contains dimensions of a contrasting better way of being: "We do not have to live this way." These insights elicit an urge to strive for a new form of being. These three dimensions of a single complex experience reflect a transcendental possibility of moral conversion.[10] The account of racism in America sets up a problem that transcends this

---

10. See LaReine-Marie Mosely, "Negative Contrast Experience: An Ignatian Appraisal," *Horizons* 41 (2014): 74–95.

or that racist action or this or that personal racist attitude. The problem lies more deeply in the objective rootedness of racism in American life and whether Christian spirituality really appreciates how pervasively racism is embedded in American society. This correlation sets up a way of explaining that Christian spirituality includes a profoundly relevant social moral conscience.

The third chapter begins the constructive argument. It dwells on racism as structural sin. The word "sin" refers to an act that is wrong, perhaps evil, and involves a personal action that includes knowledge and deliberate free agency. A person is responsible for sinful action and should feel guilty, responsible, and accountable. One stands guilty before God, not because of a known divine injunction but because of the intrinsic evil of the action, usually its injurious effect on other creatures. Given the pointed character of sin as it is traditionally understood, the phrase "structural sin" appears paradoxical, because "structure" connotes objective patterns of behavior and "sin" suggests subjective freedom and intentionality. Thus, two distinct things are discussed in the third chapter and, while not opposed, they require delicate coordination. On the one hand, structures can be sinful, not because they are sustained by any person's individual freedom but because of the corporate freedom of a society that sustains them and the participation in them by individuals. On the other hand, therefore, social responsibility is real even though it does not necessarily reach the level of being a personally responsible action. It is far easier to describe the effects of social sin than to parse the responsibility of the individuals who are involved in it. The third chapter thus shows where critical awareness of American culture and society should reorient Christian consciousness and conscience so that Christian faith can be a stronger positive anti-racist catalyst in American society than it seems to be statistically.

The fourth and fifth chapters both consider the ministry of Jesus of Nazareth: the fourth discusses Jesus as modeling the rule of God; the fifth addresses how Ignatius leads a person to appropriate the message. Jesus provides the centering form of a Christian's faith in God and of the spirituality involved in being a Christian. Both in terms of a theological conception of salvation and of a spirituality of following Jesus Christ, Jesus's ministry mediates the fundamental shape of the faith of the Christian. Jesus of Nazareth stands at the center of both being a Christian and the logic of the Spiritual Exercises. He is the hinge on which Christian faith moves in two distinct ways that are represented in these two chapters; he mediates both understanding and motivation. In the fourth chapter Jesus is presented more or less objectively as he appeared in history and how he appears in the gospels.[11] Theologically, Jesus of Nazareth was/is the revelation of God for Christian faith. More exactly, he revealed the "rule of God," a phrase that renders "the kingdom of God" in a more active and intentional way. The phrase "rule of God" also correlates with the narrative form of Jesus's ministry as the medium of his revealing. Jesus revealed God by speaking about and acting out the intention of the Creator. While the fourth chapter describes in broad strokes what Jesus stands for in objective terms, the fifth chapter contains

---

11. This book is not an appropriate place for a discussion of how one retrieves the historical figure of Jesus from the gospels. Just as Jesus was represented as an object of faith in the gospels, so too, looking back with the help of biblical scholarship, the person making the Exercises is called by Ignatius to imagine Jesus's appearance, and this can be done in a critical way.

an invitation to discipleship; it presents Jesus as one who gathered people around him and who asks the one making the Exercises to steer his or her life by a decision that either defines a commitment to the rule of God or reinforces one already in place. The backdrop for both discussions is the racism described in the second chapter.

The sixth and final chapter serves as an extended recapitulation and conclusion. It describes the union with God that may be considered the point of Christian spirituality. It draws upon some basic themes that are embedded within the final Exercise of the series proposed by Ignatius. That exercise, which bears the title "Contemplation to Attain Love," provides themes that offer an understanding of union with God that is constituted by anti-racist action. Turning to the Ignatian terms of "finding God in all things" and "contemplation in action," the concluding discussion sums up a Christian spirituality that is intrinsically anti-racist.

This overview of the argument for *Facing Race* should make it clear that this work does not resemble a manual for directing the Spiritual Exercises. Rather, by using the basic structure of the Exercises, it employs them as a way of introducing the message of the gospels in a racist situation.

I

A Theological Prelude

In 1974 Ignacio Ellacuría presented a series of lectures that summarized his interpretation of the Spiritual Exercises of Ignatius Loyola as a spiritual guide for how his fellow Jesuits might consolidate their spirituality in a way that responded to the world in which they found themselves.[1] The Spiritual Exercises have inculcated a spiritual language for Jesuits at large since the founding of the order. But the world in which Central American Jesuits lived differed considerably from the cultural context of Spain and Europe in the first half of the sixteenth century. Ellacuría felt the need for

---

1. The outlines and notes for these lectures were published as Ignacio Ellacuría, "Lectura latinoamericana de los Ejercicios Espirituales de san Ignacio," *Revista latinoamericana de teología* 23 (1991): 111–47. J. Matthew Ashley's translation of the notes was published as Ignacio Ellacuría, "A Latin American Reading of the Spiritual Exercises of Saint Ignatius," *Spiritus: A Journal of Christian Spirituality* 10, no. 2 (Fall 2010), 205–42. Ashley has also commented on these notes in "A Contemplative under the Standard of Christ: Ignacio Ellacuría's Interpretation of Ignatius of Loyola's Spiritual Exercises" in the same issue of *Spiritus*, 192–204.

the renewal called for by Vatican II and insisted upon by progressive Latin American bishops. The idea of a new appropriation of the Exercises was not simple, and Ellacuría had been working on it for some time. Over the years of his study and leadership he developed an intricate interpretation of the Exercises for his and, analogously, our time.[2]

In the first half of the twenty-first century, the United States also needs a reading of the gospel that addresses the world in which we live. In many ways, the stakes are higher than those faced by Ellacuría. On the level of society, the racism in the United States has been compared with the Holocaust as a scandal to the moral credibility of America's predominant faith tradition. On the level of culture, the churches are losing traction at a rate that indicates that either their message or their way of presenting it is deficient. As Ellacuría used the Spiritual Exercises to open up to his colleagues a spirituality that directly addressed the structural sin of systematic poverty in his land, this work uses them to address the structural sin of racism.

A theological and spiritual response to a social issue has to consider the cultural challenges to the credibility of the language it uses. The United States has become a more metaphysically skeptical, relativistic, and ontically pessimistic country than ever before. Its pragmatism does not easily accept metaphysical premises. Too many faith traditions make too many claims about what we cannot really know. In a country of great religious diversity, many Americans have become relativist or agnostic about absolute truths. The great diversity of religions that do not get along

---

2. I use the term "analogous" consistently in this work for two reasons: to avoid an easy identification of things that are really different, and to affirm a creative imagination that can find or create congruences between things that call up possibilities for the future.

together subverts all of them. And in the face of widespread human deprivation that we either tolerate or take for granted, many look with skepticism on easy affirmations about an ultimate meaning and goal of life over against just getting along in this one.[3]

This chapter addresses these issues with a brief account of where Christian language comes from. To do this in a brief space risks a level of abstraction from the enormous practical problem at hand. But at the same time, the analysis presented here is meant to be open to other faith traditions on shared humanistic grounds. It will lay the groundwork for demonstrating that anti-racism in Christianity consists of more than evangelical exhortation but belongs to the essence of Christian faith. Discussing these issues in terms of three crucial themes lays bare in skeletal form the basic logic of this book. These are, first, a consideration of the fundamental structure of Christian faith. This is presented in such a way that it correlates with other faith traditions and thus begins to build a coalition of religious faith traditions against racism. Christian theology cannot credibly exist today in a bubble. The second theme has to do with the inner nature of Christianity as a faith tradition. The point is to show that the key terms for understanding Christianity are "discipleship" and "movement" rather than "protected knowledge" and "worldview." The third theme for this theological introduction is "spirituality." The Spiritual Exercises of Ignatius Loyola are introduced as a particular spirituality that captures the essence of Christianity in a deep way that can guide the response of Christian faith as being intrinsically hostile to racism. The goal of this introductory chapter

---

3. Roger Haight, *The Nature of Theology: Challenges, Frameworks, Basic Beliefs* (Maryknoll, NY: Orbis Books, 2022), 3–21.

lies precisely there. A reaction against racism does not constitute an add-on to the Christian faith tradition but is a dimension of its substance or essence. It requires the kind of theology that Johann Baptist Metz called "a practical fundamental theology."[4]

The Structure of Christian Faith

We begin with a consideration of the inner structure of Christian faith. It consists of a way of life whose essential form has its source in the mediating ministry of Jesus of Nazareth. That foundational perspective can be drawn from a broader conception of the dynamics of revealed religion.

Much of Christian theology takes the term "revelation" for granted. But it is a contentious term from two opposite points of view. Secular culture finds it suspicious; "revelation" sometimes connotes delusions. And from a strictly religious point of view, revelation seems to fill the world with many radically different worldviews. Our world is cluttered with too much revelation or too many of them. In a straightforward framework for talking about revelation, John Smith, an American empiricist philosopher, offered a relatively simple model for understanding revelation in terms of a shared religious experience with three elementary components: it is a religious experience in which (1) a transcendent object is (2) mediated to human consciousness and (3) interpreted by those who receive it.[5] The key to this theory lies in mediation, as the following synopsis of

---

4. Johann Baptist Metz, *Faith in History and Society: Toward a Practical Fundamental Theology* (New York: Crossroad, 2007).

5. John Smith, "The Disclosure of God and Positive Religion," in *Experience and God* (New York: Oxford University Press, 1968), 68–98.

Smith's theory shows. The point here is not to teach a theology of revelation but to communicate an appreciation of the elementary structure of the Christian imagination in tune with other faith traditions. We are digging down to the core of Christian sensibility.

Revelation occurs within human experience. The distinctiveness of revelation lies in its character as an event. "The disclosure of God takes place through a historical medium."[6] To a broad sense of a religious dimension of experience, such as the experience of absolute dependence (Friedrich Schleiermacher) or the holy and wholly other (Rudolf Otto), the medium adds positive content. "Revelation means primarily the encounter of God through a medium."[7] A medium is a finite reality bearing the divine presence and pointing to it beyond itself. Smith locates revelation as a third mode of disclosure between mysticism and rationalism; one encounters transcendent reality within the medium in the way that another self is encountered in gesture and language. Bodily symbols are not necessarily the self, because they may deceive; but, like another's eyes, they may elicit a response to another authentic, transparent self. The dynamics of revelation appear in the analogy as free communication of the self in outward manifestations. Finally, revelation requires interpreters who read the media or signs and formulate expressions of their content.[8] The theory fits Christianity well; in it and in the other Abrahamic religions, the

6. Smith, "The Disclosure of God," 70.

7. Smith, "The Disclosure of God," 77.

8. Smith sums up the pattern of revelation this way: "There is the divine reality to be disclosed, there is the medium of disclosure, and there is the interpreter who reads the meaning of the disclosure in terms of the medium." "The Disclosure of God," 92.

transcendent object is personal. It also unites Christian faith with other faith traditions on the supposition that they share such a common human structure. It thus opens Christian language of liberation to conversation with other faith traditions about our common moral dilemmas.

This theory of revelation can be debated, but it becomes useful here when one turns it around and views it as a description of religious experience within the Christian tradition of beliefs. Jesus is the medium of Christian interpretation of God. Considering this proposition existentially yields basic insight into the character of participation in the Christian faith tradition. For example, Jesus first of all functions as mediator of God; he mediates an encounter with God. He has to stimulate experience of God, other than his human presence, in order to be revelatory. God is transcendent other, so that one does not have a firsthand account of God in order to test the authenticity of the revelation. One knows God in the encounter through the medium. Moreover, everyone who encounters God through Jesus will interpret God and the medium according to each one's personal condition. Beneath the objective theory one finds a living existential reality that, within a common faith tradition, remains deeply and uniquely personal. The theory of revelation also indicates a level of engagement that can be intense. In the light of this understanding of revelation, the gospel stories put Christian faith into close dependence upon its source.

Not only is the original revelation tied to history as in the events of the mediation, so too are the faith tradition and the mode of the reception at any given time. For example, to receive and interpret the revelatory message of Jesus in the United States today requires that it be absorbed into a social and cultural setting of racism. To read Jesus in exclusively individualistic personal terms cut off from social and cultural conditions short-circuits his meaning to the level of misinterpretation. Jesus was a critic of his society: "O faithless and perverse generation" (Lk 9:41). He mediated the critique of the rule of God; that has to be part of an interpretation of Jesus today.[9]

Revelation and faith relate to each other like parent and child: the one implies the other. Revelation needs faith to be complete; without faith receiving it, there would be no revelation. And faith needs revelation to have content; faith seeks transcendence, something beyond ordinary knowledge that contains all-encompassing value. The reciprocal and dialectical relationship between revelation and its reception by faith means that the dynamic character of faith forms a dimension of revelation itself. Examining faith shows how Jesus bears the presence of God into the world and, in the end, how God works in history through agents. Racism will not be overcome by God without such agents.

Paul Tillich wrote in the mid-twentieth century what has become a classic statement on the existential character of faith.[10] He combined faith's active and passive dimensions in the phrase "being grasped by ultimate concern": it is always active commitment; but it comes *to* consciousness and cannot be controlled. Borrowing from Kierkegaard, Tillich saw faith as infinite passion or a passion for the infinite. From Schleiermacher he learned that faith involves an experience of absolute dependence in being that grounds, centers, and orients a human life. Like Luther, Tillich preserves the idea of existential clinging, a fundamental moral

---

9. The phrase "the rule of God" needs further explanation, and that is offered in Chapter IV.

10. Paul Tillich, *Dynamics of Faith* (New York: Harper Torchbooks, 1958).

response that characterizes the whole of a person's life even when it escapes clear conceptual consciousness and intentionality. The description rings true to those who consider the question because it calls up deep self-reflection. When one probes the question of where one's deepest faith lies, one's attention is drawn to a layer of the self that may not be so clear. The closest one can get to personal faith requires the narrative of one's story. The Christian tradition constantly repeats it: one's real faith, like one's love, manifests itself in one's actions. This explains why we can say that everyone lives by some faith. The object of that faith lives within each one's history.

The relevance of this description of faith can be condensed into two points. The first revolves around the fact that Christian faith in God is principally mediated by Jesus of Nazareth. The foremost and grounding function of Jesus can be summed up in the idea that for Christians he mediates contact with and revelation of God. He performs this role not primarily by delivering an objective set of teachings or beliefs about God, but by communicating or mediating an encounter with the mystery of God through the conduct of his whole ministry, which is reflected fragmentarily in the New Testament gospel accounts. Jesus's ministry was itself a going around doing good that impacted people (Acts 10:38). The impact led many to conclude that God was present and active in Jesus's ministry. The "inside-out" dynamic seems straightforward; the encounter led to formulation, expression, interpretation, and reflection. And so it does today when one enters imaginatively into the gospel stories.

The second point lies within the first and draws it out. The gospels' stories are not transcripts or historically accurate descriptions of Jesus's ministry, but rather highly interpretive accounts intended to mediate a faith-encounter. Neither were they intended as the series of doctrines that they gradually generated over time. They are better described as witnesses to a way of life committed to the rule of God. They communicate both the way God relates especially to human beings and how humans in response are supposed to live in relation to God, one another, and the world. The narrative form of communication, as distinct from the didactive teaching that they include, works through interpretation that draws into itself the current context. One never simply reads meaning off the page. Because the Jesus stories of the gospels mediate the meaning of God for one's life, the filter of personal situation enters into each one's appropriation of revelation.

To recapitulate this description of the source of Christian spirituality in revelation and faith. And one can postulate a common structure among all religious faiths that rely on a historical mediation of a transcendent source. Jesus of Nazareth was/is the mediating representative of God for Christian faith. This means that the foundational form of Christian faith life draws its energy from Jesus of Nazareth. But two qualifiers attach to this basic view. The first recognizes that God, the object of faith, transcends our language about God. The second acknowledges that ultimate faith commitment lies so deep in human consciousness that the best indicator of real or actual faith lies in human behavior.

Christianity as Discipleship

The structure of revelation formulates how Jesus's ministry operated as the medium of Christian experience. In the narrative, one can learn how disciples encountered God in the world and appropriated an orienting commitment for their lives. It also illumines how Jesus's ministry may be appropriated today through an adjustment from Jesus's time to our own particular historical context. The gospel stories solicit response to what Jesus called the rule of God. In every case, the rule of God has to refer both to what Jesus meant in his context and to what it may mean in the ongoing present time of the interpreter.

When Ignacio Ellacuría proposed an interpretation of the gospel to his fellow Jesuits in Central America, he built on two foundational principles. One was that God had to be found not up above us but within the world itself. He used the term "theologal" to characterize the world that bears God within it. The other principle he called "historicization," which refers to an encounter with God in history that elicits a response to God in history, that is, through or by human activity. In what follows we expand the implications of these two insights, the first in light of the implications of the doctrine of creation for spirituality, and the second in the context of a response to racism. This section concludes with the conviction that Christianity, as a whole, should be regarded as a movement that is itself constituted by disciples.

We begin with Ellacuría's account of the two foundational principles.[11] The first term, "theologal," describes a view that sees all of reality penetrated through and through with God's presence. It may be described by theologies of creation, or grace, or incarnation and salvation, or all of

---

11. Ellacuría describes these ideas in the notes for the first of eight lectures on the Spiritual Exercises: "A Latin American Reading of the *Spiritual Exercises* of Saint Ignatius," 205–9. The two concepts reinforce each other and provide a rationale for understanding the Spiritual Exercises in the context of the secular situation of Central America at the time.

these in combination. God's presence carried by God's creating power suffuses everything. From elementary particle to the whole of the universe, in the most secular sphere and in events considered good and evil, God is there. But this presence must be understood on a level of God's creating agency and not as a rival created reality. Because God is transcendent and cannot be encountered directly, God should not be imagined as a distinct entity but can only be recognized as the power of being within all the concrete events of history. God will always be God and not creature; and people will always be creatures, unable to step out of their earthly condition and finite environment.

This leads to another reflection: God's presence and activity within the world can be clarified by the distinctions that accompany a theology of creation as the continuing support of finite being. Theology uses the phrase "out of nothing" to distinguish creation from earthly creativity (making something out of something else). In the active sense of creating, creation places God directly and immediately within all the processes of nature; they all depend on God for their very being. "Out of nothing" means there is nothing between God creating and the creature. This immanent presence of God as ongoing Creator also invites metaphorical language of God's presence in terms of power, or energy, or spirit acting rather than as a distinct physical object. The immanence of God, like God, cannot be thought of in terms that are shared by or compete with physical or finite beings. God is other, but God is present within the physical world and intimately close as its sustaining Creator.

The theology of God creating out of nothing entails God being personally present to all creation. This cannot be understood as a presence to the whole of creation, all at once, as an ongoing impersonal sustaining force. If God is personal, then God is present to each discrete element of creation as personal. This means that God's presence subsists as self-presence, one that infinitely exceeds or transcends human self-consciousness and imagination, but cannot be less than these projections. It would be hard to imagine a union closer than that of God to creatures; it is an infinite self-presence, a personal creating and sustaining of creatures, with the notation that God completely exceeds human imagination and infinitely loves what God creates.

This aspect of the doctrine of creation makes it a vital part of any conception of spirituality or relationship with God. Creation theology often finds a place in cosmological speculation and rarely reappears as practical theology. But ongoing creation entails the personal and loving presence of God to each person and each creature in the universe. Before the rudiments of the doctrine of the Trinity were formulated in the fourth century, the notion of God as Spirit, God immanent in the world and especially "manifest" as a principle of life and expanded capacities of creaturely behavior was closely associated with the same power of God within the created world. In brief, the transcendent God who totally exceeds human imagination also lives within finite creation and can be experienced indirectly or obliquely in human dependence, need, and aspiration. It will become apparent along the way that God as Presence thus bestows a value on each creature that is intrinsic to itself, in itself, and in its co-existence with other creatures. The rock-bottom principle of Christian theology that negates the white supremacy that supports racism lies in creation theology. God loves everything that God creates and bestows upon it intrinsic value.

The idea of "theologal" reality and the reflections on creation approach the borders of an experience that some might consider mystical. They express a heightened and meditative experience of the world and appreciation of it. This level of reflection indicates that the gospels do not offer a transactional relationship with either God or Jesus of Nazareth. The whole process of engagement with God involves an openness to a transcendent experience of God through earthly mediation. The whole package of revelation, faith, and religious experience entails a quality that can be called mystical.[12]

The second foundational principle governing Ellacuría's thinking is "historicization."[13] It generates different nuances according to the subject matter. It requires that any explanation of theological meaning must pass through an imagination that visualizes the historical behavior it entails or leads to, if not an actual doing. Historicization means not being satisfied with what may be a universal meaning that by definition is abstract. Abstract meaning does not adequately explain the actual meaning in a specific case or situation; that meaning has to be particular or concrete to be relevant. Historicization also suggests that an acting out of ideas in historical events serves as a criterion of their adequacy and sometimes their truth.

The tying of meaning to an actual or an imagined future keeps thinking focused on the world of actuality and performance in the manner of a historical existentialism. Historicization has direct bearing on the meaning of the gospels because they present Jesus in the narrative form of

---

12. It may be important to underline this point because an anthropomorphic instinct always tempts human reckoning with God to be conducted on the basis of ordinary human exchange. In that measure, it misses the point.

13. J. Matthew Ashley, "Ignacio Ellacuría and the Spiritual Exercises of Ignatius Loyola," *Theological Studies* 61 (2000), 24–27.

his ministry. Jesus said this or did that in a concrete moment of time. Ignatius Loyola uses the imagination to negotiate a realism in the experience of Jesus. Encounter with God in the gospels always makes God present in a way that "is not first or even primarily actualized and expressed in words,...but is enfleshed in a historically realized human life."[14] This refers to both the mediation of Jesus and the reception of relevant meaning for one's concrete life in the world. The idea of historicization thus draws together in consciousness the narrative character of Jesus's revelation and its relevance to the interpreter's present and future.

Ellacuría's ideas of God's immanence in the world and the need to "historicize" how we think about Christian faith can be expressed in another way in the abstract but telling terms of the essence of Christianity. The idea of an "essence" of Christianity has frequently been shown to be bogus when it tries to reduce a complex historical movement to a single idea. Whether in the hands of John Henry Newman or Adolf von Harnack, it always represents reductionism.[15] At the same time, after recognizing that historical reductionism is impossible, the quest for the inner logic of Christianity can be positive. Many theologians over the centuries have proposed an intrinsic consistency of the tradition. The plurality

---

14. Ashley, "Ignacio Ellacuría," 29.

15. Newman recognized that Christianity could not be reduced to or contained by a central idea, but if one considered a central idea as a matter of convenience, "to group others around it, no fault can be found with such a proceeding: and in this sense I should myself call the Incarnation the central aspect of Christianity." (Newman, *An Essay on the Development of Christian Doctrine* [Westminster, MD: Christian Classics, 1968], 36); Adolf Harnack, *What Is Christianity?* (New York: Harper Torchbooks, 1957), tried to reduce Christian faith to a core of love of God and love of neighbor that interactively reinforce each other.

of such syntheses shows that they do not have to be understood exclusively.[16] Ideal types and models not only allow but also invite realistic comparison and contrast. The point of offering a centering idea of Christianity at this point aims at simplifying theological jumble and dysfunction.

The theory of revelation described earlier helps to provide the dimensions of the essence of Christianity proposed here. It involves the three dimensions of a historical revelation: its object is God, it is mediated by Jesus of Nazareth, and it is appropriated in the power of God as Spirit. These three dimensions are formal or structural and open. In Christianity, they point to dimensions in a living faith tradition that has taken the many forms of faith to which history bears witness.

In the light of these dimensions, the essence of Christianity as a historical movement takes the form of discipleship. Jesus stands at the source of specifically Christian faith, and disciples form the bridge between Jesus in history and the movement that followed and gradually became the church. Jesus's mediation of God and faith in God cannot be shrunk to teaching about God. It included a fuller representation of the rule of God, the reciprocal relationship between God and human life, and a mode of existence in the face of God that included responsibility for one another. Jesus's mediation also included revelation of authentic human existence, a mode of life within the sphere of God's intention and rule. The basic dynamism of Christianity can thus be described in terms of discipleship of Jesus Christ. As the movement grew it generated reflection on itself that involved the

---

16. For example, H. Richard Niebuhr, *Christ and Culture* (New York: Harper, 1951), and Avery Dulles, *Models of the Church* (New York: Doubleday, 1974), use typology to show a pluralism of centering understandings of Christianity.

development of doctrines about God, Jesus, human existence, and the relations between them.[17]

In sum, the dynamics of revelation and faith yield a movement in history of disciples of Jesus. The deepest essence of Christianity does not consist of the institutions that sustain it but of the form of life that goes on within them. To be a Christian is less "being a member" and more a way of life in history that is fueled by a relationship with God. But that relationship itself has to deal with the moral dilemmas that constitute human existence.

The Spiritual Exercises as Delivery System

We conclude this theological introduction to the discussion of a Christian response to racism with a consideration of the idea of spirituality and in particular the spirituality found in the Spiritual Exercises of Ignatius Loyola. The term "spirituality" in Christianity can almost be equated with following Jesus of Nazareth, with discipleship. The bridge between the structure of Christian faith, through discipleship, to spirituality is straightforward. And the traffic passes in both directions.

On a fundamental level, spirituality is a dimension of human existence itself; religious affiliation and a Christian way of life specify more particular and finally personal com-

---

17. This model of Christianity finds support in the theology of Avery Dulles, who developed an ecumenically sensitive description of five models of the church in *Models of the Church*. Later he synthesized his earlier work with an encompassing model of the church as the "community of disciples." Avery Dulles, "Community of Disciples as a Model of the Church," *Philosophy and Theology* 1, no. 2 (Winter 1986): 99–120. In all of his work, the church is more than its various institutional forms; it is a living, pluralistic corporate movement.

mitments. The term "spirituality" thus enjoys wide usage and many different meanings depending on context. We have already briefly defined spirituality in the preface and considered the Exercises in relation to Christian spirituality in terms of discipleship and following the model of life found in the ministry of Jesus. But there is more to be said about the fundamental meaning of spirituality and how the spirituality of the Exercises relates to it. These considerations amount to a definition of terms that will take on deeper relevance in later chapters.

Spirituality may be understood in a common secular way today as a sphere of depth and reflection on the meaning of human life, one's own life in particular and the direction it is taking. Spirituality no longer automatically entails religious confession. As previously mentioned, spirituality in this work refers to the way persons and groups lead their lives in the face of what they consider ultimate reality. The dimension of ultimacy plunges ordinary behavior into a sphere of deeper and more extensive meaning. The conception aligns neatly with the structure of faith described earlier with attention to the action of living and its orientation. If spirituality can be called faith in action, as suggested earlier, then spirituality refers to the way persons manifest the convictions of their faith in their activity. Religious faith introduces transcendence into the equation of human life. Living in the face of ultimacy, of one's self-defining center of gravity, turns behavior into an expression of commitment to some supreme value.

But just as transcendence requires faith because the object exceeds the human power to grasp its character, so too does the real object of faith lie hidden in the complexity of human response. What is a person's real faith below all the confessions of loyalty? "For where your treasure is, there will your heart be also" (Matt 6:21). Such questions about subterranean motivation are easily asked and difficult to answer. Faith spreads out in human personality; it gives rise to beliefs; it requires a strong will in crisis; sometimes faith seems to just follow feeling and desire. But faith also shapes our deepest hope. In Freud's view, it expresses human need; in Augustine's, it longs for its ultimate goal. Because faith lies beneath all these layers, it may be difficult to know where our own faith is ultimately situated. Do I really have faith? I don't know, but I have to act as if I do.

The deepest container of faith and the best indicator of its character can be found in a person's behavior. To some extent, analogously, this may be partly true of groups as well. People's deepest faith lies in their actions, so that the sum total of a person's actions reveals the values that actually motivate his or her life. This applies both inside and outside of explicitly religious situations. The whole range of human activity enters into the definition of human persons and thus helps determine what commands their deepest commitment and how different elements relate to it. This theme permeates the gospels. "You will know them by their fruits. Are grapes gathered from thorns, or figs from thistles" (Matt 7:16)? Beneath the saying, which relies on common sense, lies an anthropology seldom recognized. We need to know our history just to know ourselves.

The hidden character of the depths of faith leads to a consideration of the relation between spiritual reflection and overt activity or behavior. In the domain of spirituality, this tension appears in the relation between contemplation and action. An obvious relationship obtains here; just as knowledge enables intentional human action, spiritual reflection on activity leads to self-awareness and knowledge of the world. But this formula leaves too much room for a separation between the two forms of human action and establishes a framework for alternating behaviors. A more synthetic formula holds the two together. As Paul Lakeland states it: "Belief without action is empty; but action without belief is thrashing around in the dark."[18] That axiom forces one to imagine how contemplation and action might be simultaneous. How does the depth of Christian faith that lies deep in one's behavior come to bear on everyday life?

The question of how Christian faith influences secular moral life in the world as one finds it directly occupied Ignatius Loyola and permeates the Spiritual Exercises he composed. Moreover, as noted in the preface, he drew his inspiration from the gospel stories that depicted Jesus's ministry. Our turn to the Spiritual Exercises does not deal with the way they might be adapted to particular people who engage them. On the contrary, we focus on them as providing a delivery system that shows exactly how Christian spirituality confronts racism. To address this in a short space, the discussion that follows briefly describes the text of the Spiritual Exercises, then isolates the deep structure of how they represent Christian spirituality in the face of a critical social moral issue, and finally explains how this structure guides the chapters of this book.

Ignatius of Loyola (1491–1556) was a Basque nobleman who as a teenager was sent to train as a courtier in the household of the treasurer of the Spanish crown. Later, at the age of thirty and in royal service to the viceroy of Navarre, he was wounded in battle at Pamplona in 1521 and underwent a long process of healing at the family manor in Azpeitia. There he began a protracted two-year period of conversion to

---

18. Paul Lakeland, *Freedom in Christ* (New York: Fordham University Press, 1986), 45.

the life of a pilgrim that included a time of deep introspection during which he began to compose what would become his Spiritual Exercises. The finished product, published in the 1540s, was a manual of spiritual instruction, the core of which is made up of a series of meditations to be done successively over four weeks on sin, the ministry of Jesus, the passion narratives, and the stories of Jesus's appearances. But distributed through this series of what Ignatius called "contemplations" are exercises that are typically Ignatian. These guiding contemplations and the series of commentaries and notations that are part of the volume give the Exercises proper their Ignatian character. The Spiritual Exercises became a standard vehicle of formation of the spirituality of those who entered the religious order founded by Ignatius in 1540 and many others across five centuries.

But the present discussion prescinds from the details and the complexity of the vocabulary of the Spiritual Exercises and the long tradition of their application. Our approach to the Exercises here focuses instead on their deep structure or, synonymously, their inner logic. This foundational reading of the Exercises provides the rationale for them to perform their function of being the delivery system that applies Christian faith to the social sin of racism.

Gaston Fessard's analysis of the basic structure of the Spiritual Exercises illustrates what is meant by their inner logic.[19] Evil and good are reciprocal alternatives. Good appears in contrast to evil, grace appears in contrast to sin. From

---

19. Gaston Fessard, *The Dialectic of the Spiritual Exercises of St. Ignatius of Loyola*, trans. Oliva Blanchette and James Colbert (Leiden: Brill, 2022). Édouard Pousset, *Life in Faith and Freedom: An Essay Presenting Gaston Fessard's Analysis of the Dialectic of the Spiritual Exercises of St. Ignatius* (St. Louis: Institute of Jesuit Sources, 1980) provides a more accessible presentation of Fessard's work.

the experience of evil, the turn to Jesus is to the possibility of grace: the good, grace, and being exist in contrast to evil's negation of being. In Fessard's view, the basic logic of the Exercises consists of looking into the face of evil or sin and, by contrast, looking at Jesus of Nazareth as a source of God's goodness and grace. After contemplating these contraries, the Exercises lead one to make the decision to commit one's life to the will of God as Jesus manifests it. Fessard is operating within a Hegelian framework, but one can read an analogy between his dialectic and the dynamics of a negative experience of contrast referred to in the preface. Fessard emphasizes, moreover, how Ignatius intended the Exercises to assist in all kinds of decisions for the reform of one's life (SE, 189). In effect, Ignatius universalized his own experience as the way God deals with all people. In Fessard's view, Ignatius "intended to affirm the spiritual value of his method for everyone and for all their decisions."[20] In this way Fessard read the dynamic structure of the Exercises as reflecting the inner dynamism of Christian faith itself and how it governed one's life.

Ignacio Ellacuría interpreted the core of the Exercises as having a structure analogous to the analysis of Fessard, *mutatis mutandis*. As Ashley lays it out, the basic structure has four components.

1. The first is the set-up in the first week's dwelling on human sinfulness.

2. Sin moves the Christian to turn to Jesus of Nazareth in order to encounter God's love in the ministry of Jesus. The narrative backbone of the Exercises lies in the stories that recount Jesus's ministry.

---

20. Fessard, *The Dialectic*, 98.

3. The contemplations of events in Jesus's ministry lead a person to "make a life-determining choice, fulfilling the primary goal of the Exercises: 'seeking and finding God's will in the ordering of our life for the salvation of our soul.'"[21] Ignatius calls the life-choice "an election." The considerations of the passion and the apparitions of Jesus in the third and fourth weeks of the Exercises do not add to the climax of decision and action, but they strengthen the resolve of a life-commitment.

4. Finally, the recapitulation of the Exercises is found in the concluding "Contemplation to Attain Love." This final contemplation can function not as an end or conclusion but as a vision encompassing the whole development. I consider the basic structure of the Exercises in the first three parts and use the *Contemplatio* as a reprise of the spirituality contained in the Exercises as a whole.

This deep structure of the Spiritual Exercises allows them to serve as a dynamic vehicle for showing how the inner faith commitment of Christian faith that consists of discipleship relative to Jesus elicits a way of life that contradicts and resists the social and cultural evils that affect historical human existence. The point of this is that racism in America cannot be considered one among many social ethical problems that an integral faith tradition must consider. Racism forms part of the air we breathe and thus has a negative foothold in the internal structure of faithful existence. Although it is not alone in holding such a position, it cer-

---

21. Ashley, "Ignacio Ellacuría," 20, citing SE #1.

tainly points to a contrary moral imperative subsisting within the essence of Christian faith.

This foundational theological discussion sets up a fuller account of how the chapters of the book follow this inner logic of applying the gospel to Christian faith as it is lived in America. Chapter II begins with a brief description of the racism that characterizes American culture and society. This chapter consists of reportage, appealing to the history and the present-day dynamics of racism as it is testified to by witnesses and analyzed by social and theological commentators. Its purpose is to represent the given as experienced, especially by those who are most affected by it.

Chapter III starts building a theological response by turning to the Spiritual Exercises, which begin with a consideration of sin. Ignatius devotes a good deal of time to meditation on sin in the variety of forms it takes in Christian tradition. The multiple considerations of sin culminate most sharply in personal sin as that which needs to be appropriated by anyone making the Exercises. Ignatius, like Luther, implicitly felt that God's mercy and love would be more deeply appreciated the more persons had a true sense of their sinfulness. The emphasis, therefore, falls on a personal recognition of one's own sinful condition. In contrast to this individual and personal perspective, but certainly not in contradiction to it, setting the Exercises in the context of racism addresses a sensibility of structural sin and learning how its tentacles embrace the whole of society. The burden of Chapter III thus consists in bringing out the ways in which a social situation engages personal responsibility, something especially difficult to understand in a post-Enlightenment, capitalist, and individualist environment. But at the same time, the objectivity of the analysis remains crucial because it enables Blacks and whites to talk with each other about this sensitive issue. This project represents a major modification in the interpretation of the Exercises that flowed from Ignatius's pen, one that requires a measured shift in understanding and adjustment of our language.

Chapter IV carries the same perspective forward with the question of the meaningfulness of Jesus's ministry for a situation of structural sin that is distinct from personal sin. Where and how does the ministry of Jesus find traction in contrast to the structural sin of racism that infects American life? The analysis in Chapter IV does not exclusively fall on Jesus the social critic who pointed out the collective sin of his own social and religious situation. That is important and cannot be ignored; it provides analogies for present-day application. But our analysis emphasizes in contrast to structural sin the possibilities that Jesus and his ministry open up for people and through them for the wider society. It represents the contrastive utopic vision that Jesus holds up for humankind. This accent provides connective tissue for Blacks and whites to cooperate in building a new community.

Chapter V addresses the third dimension of the inner logic of the Exercises that move toward and find a climax in a life-decision. The previous focus on the objective ministry of Jesus shifts inward to the self-before-God as mediated through Jesus. In Chapter V the dimension that is always present is highlighted: How does the person or group making the Exercises view themselves before God in the light of Jesus's mediation? The interpretation of Jesus allows Jesus to interpret those engaged in the Exercises. This viewpoint assumes the question explicitly proposed by Ignatius: What am I doing for what Jesus called the rule of God? The dynamic of interpretation implies not only a fusion of horizons of meaning but also a fusion of the narratives of Jesus and of those making the Exercises that lead them to decision, commitment, and action.

Finally, Chapter VI turns to the concluding exercise called Contemplation to Attain Love and treats it as a recapitulation. It sums up the extended program in terms of the formal adoption of a fundamental moral attitude of gratitude that expresses itself in action. Ignatius proposes a spirituality of gratitude following contemplation of the gifts entailed in creation itself and one's own existence. This stimulates the maxims about finding God in all things and becoming contemplative through an active loving response. The idea of creation and God working in the world for the benefit of creatures implies the interconnectedness of creatures and a social responsibility for the whole of God's creation. This large sentiment becomes present, serious, and urgent in response to concrete manifestations of racist discrimination and dehumanization.

With this preview of the argument, we turn now to an abbreviated description of racism in the United States.

II

Racism in America

Before we examine the intrinsic anti-racist character of Christian faith, logic requires a description of the meaning and dynamics of racism as it currently appears in the United States. One needs a description of the sin which the gospel message of Jesus of Nazareth opposes. The blunt title of this chapter announces at once its exact subject matter and the impossibility of characterizing it in a short space. The following statement barely outlines the complexities of the racial situation in which Black Americans live. The characterization may be rescued by a recognition that it falls short both as a report and as an adequate description of the experiences of those who suffer from the pervasive cultural and social power of racism.

Several distinct resources provide guidelines for characterizing racism in America. Racism began to infiltrate American society and culture four centuries ago with the beginning of slavery. It has assumed different institutional forms over the centuries. We begin this chapter by prying open the imagination to the four hundred years of race relations in the territory of the United States. The *1619 Project* has helped Americans understand how the roots of racism have grown long, deep, and tenacious.[1] Our analysis covers four periods: the prehistory of the nation, the flourishing of the slave economy, Jim Crow following the Civil War, and the civil rights movement after World War II. Three witnesses are inserted into the history to characterize three of these periods. From there the chapter hazards an interpretation of the elements and the dynamics of racism in American culture and society.

Long History and Strong Roots

It would be presumptuous for one unskilled in social analysis to propose an adequate description of something so deeply embedded in the American ethos as the dynamics of racial division.[2] The only way to communicate this social and cultural reality literarily has to work through the history and especially the particular stories. They reveal the animus beneath our disturbing past. History, too, generates different interpretations, and each of them carries different accents. The depth and complexity of the subject matter require an account of the perspective, even though the analytical description remains hopelessly schematic

---

1. Nikole Hannah-Jones, Caitlin Roper, Ilena Silverman, and Jake Silverstein, eds., *The 1619 Project: A New Origin Story* (New York: One World, 2021). Cited hereafter as *1619*.

2. A good introduction to racism in the United States is Jim Wallis, *America's Original Sin: Racism, White Privilege, and the Bridge to a New America* (Grand Rapids: Brazos Press, 2016). He defines this original sin in a forceful sentence he first used thirty years earlier: "The United States of America was established as a white society, founded upon the near genocide of another race and then the enslavement of yet another." *America's Original Sin*, 33. Wallis's work is especially valuable because it represents a white perspective on the issues.

and abstract. What follows offers a simplified representational form of a practical understanding of the racism in America through reference to its four-hundred-year history, some of its inner elements, and a description of its social and cultural dynamics. The analysis does not pretend to be an adequate account; it seeks only to indicate the racism that contextually surrounds Christian spirituality in the United States. All such efforts are interim reports.

As noted in the preface, the racism referred to here is directed toward African Americans; its historical origins took concrete form in slavery and it grew along with the early formation of the nation. A definition of racism would include features such as these: it consists of group and personal antagonism against another group of people on the basis of their belonging to another ethnic or racial group defined particularly by difference. Racism may include a power differential that disadvantages the others, even though the individual racist may not consciously possess it. It may also involve a social or cultural rationale that explains or motivates the attitudes. Racism, therefore, may include theories that describe the object of discrimination in various negative terms: historical, cultural, biological, and so on. But racism subsists in the actual discriminatory ideas, values, and behaviors that sustain it. Michelle Alexander offers a basic definition in objective terms: racism refers to "a stigmatized racial group locked into an inferior position by law and custom."[3] Other qualities will

---

3. Michelle Alexander, *The New Jim Crow: Mass Incarceration in the Age of Colorblindness* (New York: The New Press, 2020), 15. Another definition of racism comes from Camara Phyllis Jones. It refers to "differential access to the goods, services, and opportunities of society by race. Institutionalized racism is normative, sometimes legal-

appear in further analytical representations of racism in the United States.

A recounting of the history of the United States ordinarily begins with the founding fathers, after an extended preface of discoveries and initial settlements by Europeans. But the present culture and social situation of the Republic enable one to see clearly that the racial division and strife that define America began earlier. Reimagining the story of America beginning with the landing of the first slave ship in Jamestown, Virginia, throws revealing light on our national character.[4] In some ways, alluding to four centuries of history in a short space trivializes the subject matter. But the history makes the definition of racial injustice real; it cannot go unmentioned. A continuous line of coercive human repression in ever new forms began during the first one hundred and fifty years and was followed by the founding and early life of the nation, the period of Jim Crow in the wake of the Civil War, and the current civil rights movement.

---

ized, and often manifests as inherited disadvantage. It is structural, having been codified in our institutions of custom, practice, and law, so there need not be an identifiable perpetrator." Cited by Jeannine Hill Fletcher, *The Sin of White Supremacy: Christianity, Racism, and Religious Diversity in America* (Maryknoll, NY: Orbis Books, 2017), 84–85. Isabel Wilkerson, *Caste: The Origins of Our Discontent* (New York: Random House, 2020), situates racism in a larger socio-cultural structural system of caste. Caste allows one to see functional analogies between the systems of racism in the U.S., caste in India, and the Nazi dehumanization of Jews during the Third Reich.

4. Such is the aim of *The 1619 Project*. The editors and authors do not maintain it as the exclusive origin story, but as one that illumines the racial inequality that has characterized American society for four hundred years. Indigenous people in the United States would begin the story from a different perspective.

Racism in the United States began with slavery, whose motivation was driven by economic profit.[5] People were captured and sold into a slavery that translated into cheap labor in the production of cotton and sugar. The first hundred and fifty years of growth in the numbers of slaves saw the evolution of state laws that throttled the enslaved and protected the white population from rebellion. Slave owners were largely, although not completely, free to punish their slaves. In 1740 South Carolina restricted some punishments and thereby showed that they were being used: slave owners were to be fined if they "'cut out the tongue, put out the eye, castrate, or cruelly scald, burn, or deprive any slave of any limb or member.'" At the same time, the law authorized "whipping or beating with horse whip, cow skin, switch or small stick, or putting irons on, or confining or imprisoning.'"[6] Other laws declared that a person was born into slave existence. One person's being was to be the property of another's. These one hundred and fifty years established a foundational white supremacy that would go on to take new forms.

The second period includes the foundations of the nation in the Declaration of Independence, the Revolutionary War, the creation of the Constitution, and the financial prospering of the new country. The union of the colonies de-

---

5. Jeannine Hill Fletcher sees a strong support for racism in Christian theology's notion of Christian supremacy within the tradition: "The theology of Christian supremacy gave birth to the ideology of White supremacy, and that White supremacy grew from a dangerous ideology to an accepted subject position inherited by Whites." *The Sin of White Supremacy*, 5; also 28 and 39. This adds a layer of theological ideology to a rawer motive of economic gain.

6. Bryan Stevenson, "Punishment," *1619*, 279.

pended on a compromise with slave states that feared that a strong federal government could undo slavery. The Constitution and the Bill of Rights provided just enough protection that the slave states could legally defend their property. "The framers helped create a doctrine of private property strong enough to justify and enforce human trafficking."[7] Slavery reaped its greatest dividends after the invention of the cotton gin in 1793. It allowed as much cotton to be processed for the mills as could be planted and harvested. This expanded the wealth of the southern states exponentially during the first half of the nineteenth century and allowed the value of the slaves to increase along with a steady growth in their number, their individual outputs, and, as commodities, their ability to serve as collateral on loans to buy more slaves and property. "Together, cotton planters, enslaved workers in the South, wage laborers in the North, and millers and consumers from across the ocean helped fashion a new economy."[8] It also left an indelible proclivity for American capitalist culture to acquire wealth without work, use any means to that end, and produce massive inequality.

Solomon Northrup provides an outsider-insider description of life as a slave in a particular setting. Born in 1808, Northup was a Black freeman living in upstate New York. In 1841 he was lured to New York City and then to Washington, where he was drugged, kidnapped, sold into slavery, and shipped to Louisiana. He managed his release in 1853 and told his story in a detailed memoir. He describes his life on a cotton plantation in the following

---

7. Matthew Desmond, "Capitalism," *1619*, 171.

8. Desmond, "Capitalism," *1619*, 174–75.

passage that puts a fine point on the daily existence of a slave.

> The ground is prepared by throwing up beds or ridges, with the plough—back-furrowing, it is called. Oxen and mules, the latter almost exclusively, are used in ploughing. The women as frequently as the men perform this labor, feeding, currying, and taking care of their teams, and in all respects doing the field and stable work, precisely as do the ploughboys of the North.
>
> The beds, or ridges, are six feet wide, that is, from water furrow to water furrow. A plough drawn by one mule is then run along the top of the ridge or center of the bed, making the drill, into which a girl usually drops the seed, which she carries in a bag hung round her neck. Behind her comes a mule and harrow, covering up the seed, so that two mules, three slaves, a plough and harrow, are employed in planting a row of cotton. This is done in the months of March and April. … When there are no cold rains, the cotton usually makes its appearance in a week. In the course of eight or ten days afterwards the first hoeing is commenced. This is performed in part, also, by the aid of the plough and mule. The plough passes as near as possible to the cotton on both sides, throwing the furrow from it. Slaves follow with their hoes, cutting up the grass and cotton, leaving hills two feet and a half apart. This is called scraping cotton. In two weeks more commences the second hoeing. This time the furrow is thrown towards the cotton. Only one stalk, the largest, is now left standing in each hill. In another fortnight it is hoed the third time, throwing the furrow towards the cotton in the same manner as before, and

killing all the grass between the rows. About the first of July, when it is a foot high or thereabouts, it is hoed the fourth and last time. Now the whole space between the rows is ploughed, leaving a deep water furrow in the center. During all these hoeings the overseer or driver follows the slaves on horseback with a whip, such as has been described. The fastest hoer takes the lead row. He is usually about a rod in advance of his companions. If one of them passes him, he is whipped. If one falls behind or is a moment idle, he is whipped. In fact, the lash is flying from morning until night, the whole day long. The hoeing season thus continues from April until July, a field having no sooner been finished once, than it is commenced again.

In the latter part of August begins the cotton-picking season. At this time each slave is presented with a sack. A strap is fastened to it, which goes over the neck, holding the mouth of the sack breast high, while the bottom reaches nearly to the ground. Each one is also presented with a large basket that will hold about two barrels. This is to put the cotton in when the sack is filled. The baskets are carried to the field and placed at the beginning of the rows.

When a new hand, one unaccustomed to the business, is sent for the first time into the field, he is whipped up smartly, and made for that day to pick as fast as he can possibly. At night it is weighed, so that his capability in cotton picking is known. He must bring in the same weight each night following. If it falls short, it is considered evidence that he has been laggard, and a greater or less number of lashes is the penalty.

An ordinary day's work is two hundred pounds. A slave who is accustomed to picking, is punished, if he or she brings in a less quantity than that. There is a great difference among them as regards this kind of labor. Some of them seem to have a natural knack, or quickness, which enables them to pick with great celerity, and with both hands, while others, with whatever practice or industry, are utterly unable to come up to the ordinary standard. Such hands are taken from the cotton field and employed in other business. . . .

The cotton grows from five to seven feet high, each stalk having a great many branches, shooting out in all directions, and lapping each other above the water furrow. . . .

Sometimes the slave picks down one side of a row, and back upon the other, but more usually, there is one on either side, gathering all that has blossomed, leaving the unopened bolls for a succeeding picking. When the sack is filled, it is emptied into the basket and trodden down. It is necessary to be extremely careful the first time going through the field, in order not to break the branches off the stalks. The cotton will not bloom upon a broken branch. Epps never failed to inflict the severest chastisement on the unlucky servant who, either carelessly or unavoidably, was guilty in the least degree in this respect.

The hands are required to be in the cotton field as soon as it is light in the morning, and, with the exception of ten or fifteen minutes, which is given them at noon to swallow their allowance of cold bacon, they are not permitted to be a moment idle until it is too dark to see, and when the moon is full, they often-times labor till the middle of the night. They do not dare to stop even at dinner time, nor return to the quarters, however late it be, until the order to halt is given by the driver.

The day's work over in the field, the baskets are "toted," or in other words, carried to the gin-house, where the cotton is weighed. No matter how fatigued and weary he may be—no matter how much he longs for sleep and rest—a slave never approaches the gin-house with his basket of cotton but with fear. If it falls short in weight—if he has not performed the full task appointed him, he knows that he must suffer. And if he has exceeded it by ten or twenty pounds, in all probability his master will measure the next day's task accordingly. So, whether he has too little or too much, his approach to the gin-house is always with fear and trembling. Most frequently they have too little, and therefore it is they are not anxious to leave the field. After weighing, follow the whippings; and then the baskets are carried to the cotton house, and their contents stored away like hay, all hands being sent in to tramp it down. If the cotton is not dry, instead of taking it to the gin-house at once, it is laid upon platforms, two feet high, and some three times as wide, covered with boards or plank, with narrow walks running between them.

This done, the labor of the day is not yet ended, by any means. Each one must then attend to his respective chores. One feeds the mules, another the swine—another cuts the wood, and so forth; besides, the packing is all done by candlelight. Finally, at a late hour, they reach the quarters, sleepy and overcome with the long day's toil. Then a fire must be kindled in the cabin, the corn ground in the small hand-mill, and supper, and dinner for the next day in the field, prepared. All that is allowed them is corn and bacon, which is given out at the corn crib and smoke-house every Sunday morning. Each one receives, as his weekly allowance, three and a half pounds of bacon, and corn enough to make a peck of meal. That is all—no tea, coffee, sugar, and with the exception of a very scanty sprinkling now and then, no salt. . . .

When the corn is ground, and fire is made, the bacon is taken down from the nail on which it hangs, a slice cut off and thrown upon the coals to broil. The majority of slaves have no knife, much less a fork. They cut their bacon with the axe at the wood pile. The corn meal is mixed with a little water placed in the fire, and baked. When it is "done brown," the ashes are scraped off, and being placed upon a chip, which answers for a table, the tenant of the slave hut is ready to sit down upon the ground to supper. By this time it is usually midnight. The same fear of punishment with which they approach the gin-house, possesses them again on lying down to get a snatch of rest. It is the fear of oversleeping in the morning. Such an offence would certainly be attended with not less than twenty lashes. With a prayer that he may be on his feet and wide awake at the first sound of the horn, he sinks to his slumbers nightly.

The softest couches in the world are not to be found in the log mansion of the slave. The one whereon I reclined year after year, was a plank twelve inches wide and ten feet long. My pillow was a stick of wood. The bedding was a coarse blanket, and not a rag or shred beside. Moss might be used, were it not that it directly breeds a swarm of fleas.

The cabin is constructed of logs, without floor or window. The latter is altogether unnecessary, the crevices between the logs admitting sufficient light. In stormy weather the rain drives through them, rendering it comfortless and extremely disagreeable. The rude door hangs on great wooden hinges. In one end is constructed an awkward fireplace.

An hour before daylight the horn is blown. Then the slaves arouse, prepare their breakfast, fill a gourd with water, in another deposit their dinner of cold bacon and corn cake, and hurry to the field again. It is an offence invariably followed by a flogging, to be found at the quarters after daybreak. Then the fears and labors of another day begin; and until its close there is no such thing as rest. He fears he will be caught lagging through the day; he fears to approach the gin-house with his basketload of cotton at night; he fears, when he lies down, that he will oversleep himself in the morning. Such is a true, faithful, unexaggerated picture and description of the slave's daily life, during the time of cotton picking, on the shores of Bayou Boeuf.[9]

The witness of Solomon Northrup attends to the details of the daily life of a slave. The actual work seems ordinary, but its conditions change everything. Its horror lies in the complete bondage of a free, reflective human spirit. The passage does not describe a humane day's work but physical constraint and constant threat of physical pain. It describes not a day but a whole life. The treatment of individual

---

9. Solomon Northup, *12 Years a Slave: A True Story* (London: HarperCollins, Ebook Edition, 2014), 55–58.

persons differs little from the way farm animals might be treated.

Continuing our analysis, the third period begins with the presidency of Abraham Lincoln and reaches through turbulent times to just after World War II. Its gravity can be measured in the lives lost in the Civil War and the estimated 6,500 Blacks lynched by whites from the end of the Civil War to 1950, "an average of three every two weeks for eight and a half decades."[10] The story of the beginnings of Reconstruction and the crushing white reprisals after the withdrawal of troops from the South at the beginning of the Hayes administration dramatizes social revenge. Jim Crow refers to a situation as deadly as slavery itself, since brutality was no longer mitigated by ownership. As a result: "Between World War I and Vietnam, more than 6 million rural African Americans escaped the exploitation and terror of southern segregationist regimes and moved to northern cities, a mass migration that transformed the nation."[11] Neither the unions nor governmental programs aided the Black community. Nicole Hannah-Jones notes that "98 percent of the loans the Federal Housing Administration insured from 1934 to 1962 went to white Americans, locking nearly all Black Americans out of the government program credited with building the modern (white) middle class."[12]

---

10. Nikole Hannah-Jones, "Justice," *1619*, 465. It is commonly estimated that 620,000 people died in the Civil War, but others have revised it upward to 750,000.

11. Elizabeth Hinton, "From the War on Poverty to the War on Crime," *Racism in America: A Reade*r, ed. Harvard University (Cambridge, MA: Harvard University Press, 2020), 98.

12. Hannah-Jones, "Justice," *1619*, 466. "Whiteness colored the American labor movement's initial identity and governed its boundaries of solidarity, ultimately limiting its power." Desmond, "Capitalism," *1619*, 182.

By contrast, the emerging Black church provided major support in Black lives across the second and third periods. Blacks began to participate in Baptist and Methodist churches. Richard Allen (1760–1831) founded the African Methodist Episcopal Church in 1794 in Philadelphia; it was the first Black denominational church and continued to play a crucial role in resistance against slavery and the oppression of Jim Crow. With Absalom Jones, Allen also built nondenominational organizations committed to gospel values and social support. He exemplified the role that Black pastors played in combining spiritual and political leadership. The ordained pastor provided space for meeting, mobilization, and organization, and he assumed social and political leadership.[13] The politically engaged Black minister remains an important figure to this day.

W. E. B. Du Bois provides reflective commentary on this third period of Black history in the United States. Born in 1868 in Massachusetts, he earned a doctorate at Harvard in 1895 in history and social analysis. He went on to be the leading Black intellectual in the first half of the twentieth century. Writing incisively in 1903, Du Bois offered a poignant portrait of Black life in the South at the turn of the century. A collage of his reflections offers Black perspective on this reactionary time.[14]

It is doubly difficult to write of this period calmly, so intense was the feeling, so mighty the human passions that swayed and blinded men. Amid it all, two figures ever stand to typify that day to coming ages,—the one,

---

13. Anthea Butler, "Church," *1619*, 341–43.

14. The excerpts that follow are drawn from W. E. B. Du Bois, *The Souls of Black Folk* (New Haven: Yale University Press, 2015), Online Edition at the pages indicated in parentheses.

a gray-haired gentleman, whose fathers had quit
themselves like men, whose sons lay in nameless
graves; who bowed to the evil of slavery because its
abolition threatened untold ill to all; who stood at last,
in the evening of life, a blighted, ruined form, with
hate in his eyes;—and the other, a form hovering dark
and mother-like, her awful face black with the mists of
centuries, had aforetime quailed at that white master's
command, had bent in love over the cradles of his
sons and daughters, and closed in death the sunken
eyes of his wife,—aye, too, at his behest had laid her-
self low to his lust, and borne a tawny man-child to
the world, only to see her dark boy's limbs scattered
to the winds by midnight marauders riding after
"cursed Niggers." These were the saddest sights of that
woeful day; and no man clasped the hands of these
two passing figures of the present-past; but, hating,
they went to their long home, and, hating, their children's children live to-day (24).

[*On continued slavery*] For this much all men know:
despite compromise, war, and struggle, the Negro is
not free. In the backwoods of the Gulf States, for miles
and miles, he may not leave the plantation of his birth;
in well-nigh the whole rural South the black farmers
are peons, bound by law and custom to an economic
slavery, from which the only escape is death or the
penitentiary. In the most cultured sections and cities
of the South the Negroes are a segregated servile
caste, with restricted rights and privileges. Before the
courts, both in law and custom, they stand on a different and peculiar basis. Taxation without representation is the rule of their political life. And the result of

all this is, and in nature must have been, lawlessness and crime (31–32).

[*On Frederick Douglass*] Douglass, in his old age, still bravely stood for the ideals of his early manhood,—ultimate assimilation through self-assertion, and on no other terms" (39).

[*Riposte to white accusations*] If you deplore their presence here, they ask, Who brought us? When you cry, Deliver us from the vision of intermarriage, they answer that legal marriage is infinitely better than systematic concubinage and prostitution. And if in just fury you accuse their vagabonds of violating women, they also in fury quite as just may reply: The wrong which your gentlemen have done against helpless black women in defiance of your own laws is written on the foreheads of two millions of mulattoes, and written in ineffaceable blood. And finally, when you fasten crime upon this race as its peculiar trait, they answer that slavery was the arch-crime, and lynching and lawlessness its twin abortion; that color and race are not crimes, and yet they it is which in this land receives most unceasing condemnation, North, East, South, and West (81).

[*On freedom after the war*] Free! The most piteous thing amid all the black ruin of war-time, amid the broken fortunes of the masters, the blighted hopes of mothers and maidens, and the fall of an empire,—the most piteous thing amid all this was the black freedman who threw down his hoe because the world called him free. What did such a mockery of freedom mean? Not a cent of money, not an inch of land, not a mouthful of victuals,—not even ownership of the rags on his back. Free! (110).

Du Bois also analyzed the relationship between Blacks and whites in the South in 1900 under four headings: physical proximity, economic relations, political activity, and cultural relations. As to living space, every town and city created a physical line that separated the races; they lived apart. Economically, slavery trained Blacks in dependency. Before very long after the war, a new form of debt-slavery took over: crops, tools, clothes, and food were subject to mortgage or lien, and only a few Blacks were not under water. Politically, they were deprived of the vote; in a competitive situation this placed them at the mercy of the stronger. A slave system reduced the need for police; after the war, policing followed a dual system of leniency for whites and severity for Blacks. Funding for education favored whites three to one. In terms of culture, the life of society divided into two, like the quiet parting of a river into two streams. The color-line was drawn, each with stereotypes of the other (123–41). "In a world where a social cigar or a cup of tea together means more than legislative halls and magazine articles and speeches,—one can imagine the consequences of the almost utter absence of such social amenities between estranged races, whose separation extends even to parks and street-cars" (139).

Moving to the post–World War II civil rights movement during the fourth period, one has to begin with the fact that more than a million Black veterans were denied the benefits of the GI Bill that supported home buying and education and drew large numbers of white Americans into the middle class. Blacks were not formally excluded, but regional racism in the North and the South blocked the participation of all but a few of them.

No one represented the new quest for recognition of basic citizen rights better than Martin Luther King Jr. when, fresh from doctoral studies and installed as a pastor, he was drafted to lead the struggle. Not everyone accepted his theory and discipline of non-violence; his murder in 1968 seemed to negate their effectiveness. Many were convinced that the urban violence before and after his assassination were the only way to make white power pay attention. Today America witnesses more peaceful demonstrations, like "Black Lives Matter," and leaders in the mold of King, like Raphael Warnock. But we still walk on the razor's edge of Martin and Malcolm on the decisive balance of the alternatives of reconciliation or reciprocation depicted by James Cone.[15] We'll come back to this. But first the witness of Isabel Wilkerson.

Isabel Wilkerson is a journalist who in 2020 published an extensive structural analysis of racism as a legacy of slavery that exists today. Using the category of "caste," she compares the structure of the slavery and racism of the American South, the caste system in India, and the caste system relative to Jews during the Third Reich in Germany from 1933 to 1945. The passages that follow are drawn from her analysis of the eight pillars or foundations of caste, slavery, and racism.[16] These tenets or principles support the

---

15. James Cone, "Two Roads to Freedom," in *Martin & Malcolm & America: A Dream or a Nightmare* (Maryknoll, NY: Orbis Books, 1991), 244–71.

16. Wilkerson, *Caste*, at the pages indicated in parentheses.

socio-cultural systems that operate in the collective subconscious of those involved in them.

1. [*Divine will and the laws of nature*] "The United States and India would become, respectively, the oldest and the largest democracies in human history, both built on caste systems undergirded by their reading of the sacred texts of their respective cultures. In both countries, the subordinate castes were consigned to the bottom, seen as deserving of their debasement, owing to the sins of the past" (104).

2. [*Heritability*] "To work, each caste society relied on clear lines of demarcation in which everyone was ascribed a rank at birth, and a role to perform, as if each person were a molecule in a self-perpetuating organism. You were born to a certain caste and remained in that caste, subject to the high status or low stigma it conferred, for the rest of your days and into the lives of your descendants. Thus, heritability became the second pillar of caste" (105). One cannot ascend out of the status by achievement.

3. [*Endogamy and the control of marriage*] "The framers of the American caste system took steps, early in its founding, to keep the castes separate and to seal off the bloodlines of those assigned to the upper rung. This desire led to the third pillar of caste—endogamy, which means restricting marriage to people within the same caste. This is an ironclad foundation of any caste system, from ancient India, to the early American colonies, to the Nazi regime in Germany. Endogamy was brutally enforced in the United States for the vast

majority of its history and did the spade work for current ethnic divisions" (109).

4. [*Purity versus pollution*] "The fourth pillar of caste rests upon the fundamental belief in the purity of the dominant caste and the fear of pollution from the castes deemed beneath it. Over the centuries, the dominant caste has taken extreme measures to protect its sanctity from the perceived taint of the lower castes. Both India and the United States at the zenith of their respective caste systems, and the short-lived but heinous regime of the Nazis, raised the obsession with purity to a high, if absurdist, art" (115). The concern for purity manifests itself in Blacks being forbidden to swim in public pools, in ways of measuring racial "blood," in relegating designated castes of people to certain defining roles or jobs. "Their exclusion was used to justify their exclusion. Their degraded station justified their degradation. They were consigned to the lowliest, dirtiest jobs and thus were seen as lowly and dirty, and everyone in the caste system absorbed the message of their degradation" (129).

5. [*Occupational hierarchy*] "African-Americans, throughout most of their time in this land, were relegated to the dirtiest, most demeaning and least desirable jobs by definition. After enslavement and well into the twentieth century, they were primarily restricted to the role of sharecroppers and servants—domestics, lawn boys, chauffeurs, and janitors. The most that those who managed to get an education could hope for was to teach, minister to, attend to the health needs of, or bury other subordinate-caste people" (132–33).

6. [*Dehumanization and stigma*] "Dehumanize the group, and you have completed the work of dehumanizing any single person within it. Dehumanize the group, and you have quarantined them from the masses you choose to elevate and have programmed everyone, even some of the targets of dehumanization, to no longer believe what their eyes can see, to no longer trust their own thoughts. Dehumanization distances not only the out-group from the in-group, but those in the in-group from their own humanity. It makes slaves to groupthink of everyone in the hierarchy. A caste system relies on dehumanization to lock the marginalized outside of the norms of humanity so that any action against them is seen as reasonable" (141–42). To this she adds: "Individuals were no longer individuals. Individuality, after all, is a luxury afforded the dominant caste. Individuality is the first distinction lost to the stigmatized" (142).

7. [*Terror as enforcement, cruelty as a means of control*] "The only way to keep an entire group of sentient beings in an artificially fixed place, beneath all others and beneath their own talents, is with violence and terror, psychological and physical, to preempt resistance before it can be imagined. Evil asks little of the dominant caste other than to sit back and do nothing. All that it needs from bystanders is their silent complicity in the evil committed on their behalf, though a caste system will protect, and perhaps even reward, those who deign to join in the terror" (151). This describes both the years of slavery and in the South during the Jim Crow era.

8. [*Inherent superiority versus inherent inferiority*] "Beneath each pillar of caste was the presumption and continual reminder of the inborn superiority of the dominant caste and the inherent inferiority of the subordinate. It was not enough that the designated groups be separated for reasons of 'pollution' or that they not intermarry or that the lowest people suffer due to some religious curse, but that it must be understood in every interaction that one group was superior and inherently deserving of the best in a given society and that those who were deemed lowest were deserving of their plight" (160).

The broad analysis presented here is based on an analogy between different historical regimes and offers a synoptic, imaginative view, a sweeping horizon of comparison, that provides a deep look into human nature and motivation on the social and cultural levels. This historical account of racism invites one to try to understand the elements that comprise it. The distinctions made here represent efforts to understand its constitutive dimensions and how they work together.

The Elements of Racism

Once again, prose falls far short of the goal of understanding such a massive group consciousness as racism. It has too many foci, degrees, and conditions. This effort will be more effective as an invitation to consider the matter than as a thorough analysis. It looks for inner structures or patterns of response rather than individually conscious motivations. Objectifying these structures enables conversation. Addressing objective patterns of experiences and perceptions fosters exchange. Several different elements seem to be at work in hostile attitudes toward people of another race in a list that is far from exhaustive.

A first element consists of a projection of significant difference on another. Instead of saying the other person is not a tree or a crocodile, but a human being just like me, I notice difference. Because we like our own as those whom we know, the other becomes a candidate for suspicion. The ways of measuring attraction or repulsion to otherness are many. We may be attracted or repelled by body-type or skin color or degree of intelligence or an unknown something. We may be put off by any difference of an individual and then project it on a group, as in the insider-outsider standing in many different communities of belonging. Alienation works in the opposite direction of all the principles of attraction. Because one tends to extrapolate personal psychological analysis on groups, one can find endless reasons for corporate hostility and, of course, friendship.

Another element of racism finds its roots in the way people use language and can mistakenly take the further step of stereotyping. An oversimplified but graphic view of the formation of language describes it as a construction of public symbols to communicate experiences, reactions, and ideas in a more or less unified way by a group. Once established, the words and their meanings double back on the group and filter interpretation. To stereotype a reality or person or set of people appends a usually negative and unwarranted characteristic to an entire group of objects or persons. Cities are always dangerous; country folk are always simple; Blacks always possess criminal inclinations. Elizabeth Hinton explains the process as a version of the fallacy of making a general judgment from a single instance. The social analogue moves from statistical to universal discourse: one objectifies statistical ratios into objective qualities.[17] The formation of stereotypes represents common behavior because it works within the patterns of basic linguistic interpretation. It can be so spontaneous and routine that it becomes unnoticed and, in fact, invisible among groups.

Deep down in the heart of racism in the United States lies white supremacy. Racism thrives on otherness and categorization or branding; but the interpretation of whites as superior constitutes the bedrock of racism. The slave trade did not kidnap Europeans but those who shared an unknown language, culture, and appearance. They also lacked Western weapons. The day the first slave disembarked in Jamestown, white supremacy was institutionalized in America. The slaves were commodified and owned, and, as property, they were less than those who owned them. After four hundred years, that supremacy still exists in ways that are not perceived as such but remain operative in the resonance of language, the feeling of a situation, the quiet work of the stereotype, and the implied conclusion of so many references and spontaneous associations. Like all intersubjective exchanges, white supremacy has enough subtleties and degrees to put everyone on guard.

Willie James Jennings links white supremacy with colonialism. Modern colonialism correlates with white supremacy to form a drive toward domination, conquest, and mastery within its sphere of power.[18] He situates white

---

17. Hinton, *Racism in America*, 105–6.

18. Willie James Jennings, "Teaching and Living toward a Revolutionary Intimacy," in *"You Say You Want a Revolution?" 1968–2018 in Theological Perspective*, ed. S. P. Babka, E. P. Foley, and S. Yocum (Maryknoll, NY: Orbis Books, 2019), 13. Essays by SimonMary A. Aihiokai and Karen B. Enriquez follow the link between white supremacy and colonialism in *"Why We Can't Wait": Racism and the*

supremacy in a world premised on zero-sum competition between winners and losers. In the world of white supremacy, "whiteness" has the feel of normality; it describes the natural way of being. "Whiteness thus presents itself as skin and not as clothing."[19] Analogues to this domineering sense of whiteness may be found in forms of nationalism and other consuming ethnic or cultural identities. These comparisons help to show how readily group identities can constrict human consciousness.

Another way of identifying racism consists in regarding it as an ideology. Rather than being an individual's opinion, a collective ideology projects an objective situation and accounts for it by putting the reason for the position of Blacks within themselves. "In the eyes of most Whites, for instance, evidence of racial disparity in income, wealth, education, incarceration, and other matters becomes evidence that there is something wrong with minorities themselves."[20] This ide-

---

Church, ed. C. Punsalan-Manlimos, T. S. Tiemeier, and E. T. Vasko (Maryknoll, NY: Orbis Books, 2023).

19. Jennings, "Teaching and Living," 16. To the white supremacist, the dominant place is not gained, put on, or attributed but an internal quality of being and nature.

20. Eduardo Bonilla-Silva, *Racism without Racists: Color-Blind Racism and the Persistence of Racial Inequality in America* (New York: Rowman & Littlefield, 2018), 233. Joe R. Faegin calls this bias the "white racial frame": it is "an overarching white worldview that encompasses a broad and persisting set of racial stereotypes, prejudices, ideologies, images, interpretations and narratives, emotions, and reactions to language accents, as well as racialized inclinations to discriminate." *The White Racial Frame: Centuries of Racial Framing and Counter-Framing* (New York: Routledge, 2020), 11. He adds: It is "more than a way of interpreting the world; it typically becomes central to a white person's way of life, to their character. Whites shape their lives and actions from within it" (25).

ology formed part of the European legacy of the original col-
onization of America. Here whiteness becomes an unconscious premise and framework for appraising others; it
envelops the perception of others and thus materializes difference as a kind of reflex.[21]

And so we come to the carriers of racism. The whole
analysis up to this point has moved from the subjective aspects of racism to its public expression, whether it be language or patterns of behavior. In his popular book, *How to
Be an Antiracist*, Ibram Kendi stresses the objective policies
that effect the discrimination against Blacks. "One either believes problems are rooted in groups of people, as racist, or
locates the roots of problems in power and policies, as an
antiracist."[22] Kendi's idea is to "focus on power instead of
people" and to concentrate "on changing policy instead of
groups of people."[23] I believe that that accent is right; it allows for analysis and conversation about the subject matter
rather than each other. But it cannot exclude subjective intent or larger cultural buy-in by groups more or less affected
by racism. People have to become responsible for the motivations that are actually driving their lives.

In concluding this brief probe into the elements of
racism we need to be clear about the visible and the invisible aspects of this pervasive social and cultural disease.

---

21. SimonMary A. Aihiokai, "Deconstructing the Myth of Whiteness: A Decolonial Turn to a Eucharistic Humanity," in *"Why We Can't
Wait,"* ed. Punsalan-Manlimos, Tiemeier, and Vasko, 7–13.

22. Ibram X. Kendi, *How to Be an Antiracist* (New York: One
World, 2019), 9. One of Kendi's goals is to overcome stereotypes.
"Whenever the antiracist sees individuals behaving positively or negatively, the antiracist sees exactly that: individuals behaving positively or negatively, not representatives of whole races" (105).

23. Kendi, *Antiracist*, 11.

From one point of view, racism in America is all around us, in our history and our present divisions. It is "in-your-face" visible. But at the same time, as Michelle Alexander rightly concludes, the systems of racism are "embedded" in American society and culture. This means that sometimes it is virtually invisible because it is hidden within a maze of patterned behavior and rationalizations that make it seem normal.[24] "The unfortunate reality we must face is that racism manifests itself not only in individual attitudes and stereotypes, but also in the basic structure of society."[25]

The Dynamics of Racism

There may not be a clear line separating the elements and the dynamics of racist consciousness latent in the structures. But the distinction invites a shift toward imagining the processes that channel human reactions on a social level. How should we understand the social and psychological mechanisms that govern racist give and take? The

---

24. Alexander, *The New Jim Crow*, 14. Karen B. Enriquez describes the invisibility of whiteness as the cultural "insidiousness of the legacy of colonialism and white supremacy in this country." It pervades the social imagination and is, practically speaking, inescapable. It depersonalizes others, divests them of equality, and cannot be eradicated before it is at least recognized. Karen B. Enriquez, "Whiteness, White Christian Privilege, and Decolonizing the Academy," in *"Why We Can't Wait,"* 16.

25. Alexander, *The New Jim Crow*, 228. Alexander provides an example of her conviction: "Mass incarceration has been normalized, and all the racial stereotypes and assumptions that gave rise to the system are now embraced (or at least internalized) by people of all colors, from all walks of life, and in every major political party" (225).

term "dynamics" points to the relational interactions that help explain corporate racist consciousness and behavior. But, as in our discussion of elements, the investigation here fixes on underlying structures that apply to different cases.

We begin with an elementary description of how racism gets passed down as a cultural tradition. Bryan Massingale expresses this accurately in a single thesis: "Race functions as a largely unconscious or preconscious frame of perception, developed through cultural conditioning and instilled by socialization."[26] For those coming of age, it is the world as they find it.

An aspect of the dynamics of racism appears in groups that are opposing each other in a zero-sum game. Unlike, for example, horseback riding with others, a zero-sum game involves competition and keeping score, so that in the end there are winners and losers. It generates an appraisal of a relationship: as one side thrives the other side loses. Heather McGhee brings this to the surface from her extensive analysis of different racist scenarios. "Many white Americans view race as a zero-sum game: there's an us and a them, and what's good for them is bad for us. This rationale animates our public policies even today, when those who benefit from our country's drastic economic inequality sell the zero-sum story to block public support for any collective action that could benefit all of us, from universal healthcare to living wages."[27] In short, gain for one group is loss for another. The idea repeats itself across the

---

26. Bryan Massingale, *Racial Justice in the Catholic Church* (Maryknoll, NY: Orbis Books, 2010), 26.

27. Heather McGhee, *The Sum of Us: What Racism Costs Everyone and How We Can Prosper Togethe*r (New York: One World, 2021), study guide question, no page number.

history of racial interaction and takes on analogous forms in different situations. The basic notion is that the races are competing with each other for resources; that people of color, in their rise out of slavery, "are taking jobs from white people is another zero-sum belief that lumbers on from era to era."[28]

Max Scheler's analysis of *ressentiment* also helps in understanding the dynamics of racism insofar as it applies to the reactions of white Americans resisting and blocking the advance of Blacks. Scheler identified a number of emotional components within *ressentiment*: "The emotions and affects primarily concerned are revenge, hatred, malice, envy, the impulse to detract, and spite."[29] Some features of this deep-seated attitudinal response show its relevance. It is based on particular experiences of affront, challenge, aggression, or insult. But these feelings become repressed when they cannot be acted out, for whatever reason. Reinforced by frustration, *ressentiment* digs in more deeply and becomes more diffuse so that it affects a wider range of a person's or group's purview. Another feature is that ressentiment engages self-identity. Deep down, one's self is mixed up in resentment. *Ressentiment*

---

28. McGhee, *The Sum of Us*, 233. Frederick Douglass was fully aware of the fallacy of zero-sum logic in 1865 when he challenged whites in these practical terms: "Knowledge is power, and you have knowledge: Wealth is influence, and you have wealth. Majorities rule under our form of government, and you are the majority." Cited by David W. Blight, *Frederick Douglass: Prophet of Freedom* (New York: Simon & Schuster, 2018), 447, with reference at 823.

29. Max Scheler, *Ressentiment*, ed. Lewis A. Coser, trans. William W. Holdheim (New York: Free Press of Glencoe, 1961), 46. Scheler used the French word for resentment because it released more connotations than the German word.

"is not directed against transitory attributes, but against the other person's very essence and being."[30] The tension between the feeling of being diminished and the inability to redress the situation creates a dynamic intensity with wide application.[31]

Scheler's analysis illumines American racism in a number of ways. It reflects the close social bond between Blacks and whites in the United States. Neither group can fully understand itself apart from the other. This reciprocal relationship, the closeness, the difference, the hostility, and the constant tension in the historical interconnection invites a look at the category of social *ressentiment*, applying to white backlash against Black rising. White self-consciousness in America from the beginning of the slave trade embodies a conviction of white supremacy. American white supremacy flowered as a direct historical legacy of the institution of slavery that was then compounded after the Civil War and emancipation. *Ressentiment* fairly accurately describes the motivation of Jim Crow. It explains the constant theme that Heather McGhee found in her study of town politics and the dynamics of the trade unions. In brief, white supremacy is being challenged in a way that has become recognized within the white community. If it is still too early to affirm that real progress has been made here,[32]

---

30. Scheler, *Ressentiment*, 75.

31. See Scheler on the scope of resentment in *Ressentiment*, 69–70.

32. The idea of progress in race relations has to be examined. "The long sweep of America has been defined by two forward motions: one force widening the embrace of Black Americans and another force maintaining or widening their exclusion. The duel between these two forces represents the duel at the heart of America's racial history." Ibram X. Kendi, "Progress," *1619*, 439. Two contrasting reasons counsel against easy acceptance of progress: the appearance of progress lies

the reason lies in the depth of white supremacy and white *ressentiment*.[33]

Resentment drives an aggressive and virulent form of racism, but other more passive forms may be lodged in ignorance. Black and white cultures have been siloed and concealed from each other. This may be illustrated with the term "colorblindness." White individuals may self-describe as colorblind to indicate that race never enters into their relationships. The ordinary triggers of antipathy have no hold on these persons' relationships. But if one transfers "colorblindness" to the sphere of social existence, its bland serenity turns negatively into inattentiveness to social situation and cultural distinctiveness. One should notice Black identity as Black. Michelle Alexander has shown that racism is sustained as much by indifference as by existential bigotry. "This system of control depends far more on *racial indifference* (defined as a lack of compassion and caring about race and people belonging to certain racial groups) than racial hostility."[34] She is recalling the objectification of policy and pattern in social forms that so insert racism into society that it appears normal. "The notion that all racial caste systems are necessarily predicated on a desire to harm other racial

---

in a visibly expanding Black middle class, but it contrasts with massive statistics of social deprivation. The language of progress thus sends a wrong message.

33. Leslie and Michelle Alexander make the case that a commanding motivation for white racism lies in fear of rebellion and retaliation. "There has never been a time in United States history when Black rebellions did not spark existential fear among white people, often leading to violent response." It has shown itself in "white vigilantes, militia groups, and the police, often culminating in the creation or strengthening of systems of racial and social control." Leslie Alexander and Michelle Alexander, "Fear," *1619*, 101.

34. Alexander, *The New Jim Crow*, 252.

groups, and that racial hostility is the essence of racism, is fundamentally misguided."[35] She believes that racist systems thrive more on racial indifference than on racial animus.

The point involved in colorblindness can be made in stronger terms. The new form of racism after Jim Crow can be called "colorblind racism." To understand this phrase, one has to view racism as a social system of values and behaviors, a more or less institutionalized set of behaviors as distinct from the feelings of individuals. Eduardo Bonilla-Silva thus conceives "a society's racial structure as the totality of the social relations and practices that reinforce white privilege."[36] On a social level, racism includes the concrete patterns of behavior across all phases of social life that define the actual relationships between groups. On a cultural level, these actions include an implicitly or explicitly conscious, "loosely organized set of ideas, phrases, and stories that help Whites justify contemporary white supremacy."[37]

Colorblind racism correlates with another mistaken judgment that segregation has been finally overcome by legislation. The walls between Blacks and whites have not been torn down, neither socio-politically nor, more importantly, culturally. This is evident in the geography of race "that continues to separate us, keeping us in different neighborhoods, schools, and churches and keeping us from talking more deeply together and developing the *empathy* and *relationships* that bring understanding, friendships, common citizenship, and even spiritual fellowship."[38] A contrast with Germany, which deliberately

---

35. Alexander, *The New Jim Crow*, 252.

36. Bonilla-Silva, *Racism without Racists*, 9.

37. Bonilla-Silva, *Racism without Racists*, 233.

38. Wallis, *America's Original Sin*, 198.

keeps alive the memory of the Holocaust, illustrates this. A public opinion poll in the United States recently "surveyed high school seniors from across the country and found that only 8 percent knew that slavery was a primary cause of the Civil War."[39] Up until recently many Americans were ignorant of "the central role that slavery and anti-Blackness played in the development of our society and its institutions."[40] There are gaps on all sides: between scholarship and general knowledge; between attention to the founding fathers of the nation and the prehistory of the Union and the defense of slavery; between an estimate of normal life in America and ignorance of the lingering effects of slavery on society and culture; between different cultural lifestyles ignorant of each other.[41] In a common effort against racism, whites have to examine their participation in racist systems. "To go along with racist institutions and structures,... to just quietly go about our personal business within institutional racism is to participate in white racism."[42]

---

39. McGhee, *The Sum of Us*, 244. McGhee insists that racism is not a byproduct of non-racial forces; it cannot be rationalized exclusively by objective events; one cannot explain racism without involving participation in it by whites (229). This seems obvious enough. But it signals the need for careful analysis when we begin speaking of structural sin in the following chapter.

40. Hannah-Jones, "Preface: Origins," *1619*, xxi. A 2019 Yale study "found that most Americans believe that Black households hold $90 in wealth for every $100 held by white households. The actual amount is $10" (470). Both the gap and the ignorance are enormous.

41. Hannah-Jones, "Preface: Origins," *1619*, xxii.

42. Wallis, *America's Original Sin*, 49. He adds: "Racism in white institutions must be challenged and eradicated by white people and not just by black people. In fact, white racism is primarily a white responsibility" (50).

Beneath the social manifestations of racism, the under-side of racism consisting of the toll it takes on personal lives also calls for attention. Resmaa Menakem is a healer who analyzes and treats racism on a psychosomatic and social level. He makes two moves that provide a deeper penetration into the effects of racism.[43] First, he treats people who suffer trauma, which ordinarily refers to shocking events and condensed experiences that leave lasting personal effects. He traces traumatic distress to physiological responses of self-protection as distinct from rational, cognitive dealing with the world. Second, he shows how trauma cannot be limited to isolated sudden events, but can also be detected in the constant threatening and stressful influence of social patterns of existence. He thus changes the ordinary meaning of "trauma" and shows how the lived conditions of pervasive racist interactions perceived as dangerous can traumatize individuals and even groups.[44] As in the case of "colorblindness," a social perspective opens up new meanings and dimensions of reality.

One can see such a mechanism at work in the effects of the evolution of the American justice system as it turned its attention to urban crime beginning in the 1960s and ending up in a situation where police appear to be hunting Black males. The statistics of Black incarceration and relationship

---

43. Resmaa Menakem, *My Grandmother's Hands: Racialized Trauma and the Pathway to Mending Our Hearts and Bodies* (Las Vegas: Central Recovery Press, 2017).

44. This perspective leads to a therapeutic approach to racism that introduces new psychosomatic assumptions: "Our bodies don't care about logic, truth, or cognitive experience. They care about safety and survival. They care about responding to a perceived threat, even when that threat is not real. As a result, our bodies scare the hell out of each other." Menakem, *My Grandmother's Hands*, 28.

with the penal system outside of prison are astonishing. They are equally ineffective, except in setting up a collective insecurity among Black male teenagers and their families who are terrified of the very social system established to ensure their social safety.[45]

An Interim Conclusion

Coleman Hughes has suggested that we are offered two different visions of how to approach constructive thinking about race in the United States.[46] Martin Luther King Jr. exemplified the first in his 1963 address "I Have a Dream." In that address he appeals to American ideals of the melting pot when white and Black can unite in the beloved community. His sources are the founding documents of the nation, the Declaration of Independence and the Constitution, and the Emancipation Proclamation one hundred years before his speech. He recalls the rights of all citizens and hails the

---

45. From the personal testimony of Black teenagers in the *New York Times* documentary entitled "A Conversation about Growing Up Black," one can learn in five minutes what they face. https://www.youtube.com/watch? v=rSAw51caEeg. The relentlessness with which racism spawns new forms in changing circumstances has generated an Afropessimism among Black thinkers. It maintains the thesis that the language of political hope for the African American community is illusory. See Calvin Warren, "Black Nihilism and the Politics of Hope," *The New Centennial Review* 15, no. 1 (2015), 215–48. Also, Frank B. Wilderson III, "Afropessimism and the Ruse of Analogy: Violence, Freedom Struggles, and the Death of Black Desire," in *Antiblackness*, ed. Moon-Kie Jung and João H. Costa Vargas (Durham, NC: Duke University Press, 2021), 37–59.

46. Coleman Hughes, "A Better Anti-Racism," Persuasion (August 19, 2020), https://www.persuasion.community/p/a-better-anti-racism.

common ideals as promissory notes for national existence. He states that Blacks and whites are welded together: we cannot stand alone. He roots his dream of Black and white boys and girls together in schools as the American dream. The second vision appeals explicitly to a pluralist society where differences are noticed, tolerated, cherished, and nurtured. It calls for race-consciousness that appreciates the differences of cultures and wants to preserve them with self-conscious deliberation.

Hughes believes that the "race-consciousness" ideal will always fail because it will always be divisive. But this casts an equal suspicion that King's ideal of the beloved community, given our history, will always tend toward assimilationism. We seem to be condemned to working with both of these lofty types at the same time. The one thing that is documented in McGhee's work appears as a consistent lament: racism serves no good purpose. Neither group benefits from it.

We have thus arrived at where we must begin. Racism characterizes the American situation: we cannot escape it. It will yield only to steady work in society over a long period of time. King and Hughes provide horizons for the effort. But we cannot even move forward to consider the Christian life according to the gospel without first recognizing how deeply we are mired in our context.[47]

We are trapped in this racist situation, Black and white together. But, as Du Bois said pointedly, Blacks did not put us here. They do not hold the key to the lock. Blacks and whites

---

47. One of the reasons for insisting on the objective structural character of racism lies in escapist logic offered by the reduction of racism to conscious acts of prejudice. It allows one to deny participation in racism because "I don't do those things."

together, but the burden falls to whites. James Baldwin, who did not shy away from blunt speech, put it more dramatically than Du Bois: "What white people have to do is try to find out in their hearts why it was necessary for them to have a nigger in the first place. Because I am not a nigger. I'm a man. If I'm not the nigger here, and if you invented him, you the white people invented him, then you have to find out why. And the future of the country depends on that. Whether or not it is able to ask that question."[48]

No individual can opt out of or transcend our sociocultural condition. We are in it, and it is in us. We can only acknowledge and respond. If one ignores it, it does not go away. The attempt to prescind from it or go around it responds to it. But there is no exit.

Shawn Copeland provides a fitting conclusion to this portrait of racism in America with an invitation to a common quest for justice. "The black struggle for authenticity is coincident with the human struggle to *be* human and reveals *black-human-being* as a particular incarnation of universal finite human being."[49] The arch of justice encompasses all human beings and calls forth a common human existence and an intrinsic need for solidarity and compassion. Copeland reminds us of the value of all human persons who become actual within so many particular fleshly forms and shapes. The civil rights movement rests on a conception of human existence that reacts against individualism and domination. "If personhood is now understood to flow from

---

48. James Baldwin, *I Am Not Your Negro: A Major Motion Picture Directed by Raoul Peck* (New York: Vintage Books, 2017), cited by Mallory Yu at https://www.npr.org/2017/02/03/513311359/i-am-not-your-negro-gives-james-baldwins-words-new-relevance.

49. M. Shawn Copeland, *Enfleshing Freedom: Body, Race, and Being* (Minneapolis: Fortress Press, 2100), 21.

formative living in community rather than individualism, from the embrace of difference and interdependence rather than their exclusion, then we can realize our personhood only in solidarity with the exploited, despised, poor 'other.' In this praxis of solidarity, the 'other' retains all her (and his) 'otherness.'"[50]

In the chapters that follow we take up the gospel message of Jesus of Nazareth as it was filtered through the imagination of the Spiritual Exercises of Ignatius Loyola. Our discussion will focus on a foundational logic that might help shape Christian attitudes to the situation. It will not be about particular patterns of personal behavior whose roots can be isolated and then torn out of one's life. That should not be disparaged, of course, and many programs are addressing that practical personal need. But we also have here an objective situation that persists, in which we live, which constantly exerts its influence on the way we live, and to which we are always responding. It is prior to intentional actions. What is sought here addresses the foundational Christian vision of life from which new behaviors might flow. A theological reflection looks toward the fundamental moral commitments that should govern all Christian actions.

---

50. Copeland, *Enfleshing Freedom*, 89.

III

Racism as Structural Sin

The Spiritual Exercises of Ignatius Loyola often begin with a meditation on the Principle and Foundation of life (SE, 23). Although not technically the first exercise, it functions as such because of its careful formulation and cosmic scope. The rest of the First Week engages sin in different forms found in the tradition. Gradually attention becomes focused on one's history of personal sins. An examination of conscience may isolate certain sinful tendencies that further promote a thorough knowledge of the sinful side of the self.

Individual personal sin, not without larger metaphysical, environmental, and social spheres of temptation, preoccupy Ignatius in the First Week of the Exercises. The qualities of an individual's sin, in one's history, habits, desires, and temptations, fall within the range of personal responsibility. By contrast, the interpretation of the Exercises that follows refocuses the imagination on structural sin, where it is difficult or impossible carefully to calibrate the measure of one's participation.[1] Structural sin differs from

---

1. The idea of "structural" sin will be discussed further on. It appears with different names in theological literature: "social sin," "cor-

formally personal sin in the degree of the latter's being controlled by personal intention and decision. Personal sin always involves subjective willing and responsibility. By contrast, the idea of "structural sin" points to something objective and real whether or not an individual is aware of it. Because of its extensiveness, by definition structural sin is more devastating in its effects than the ordinary sins of individuals. Despite its objectivity, one cannot say that, because it has become a function of corporate rather than individual human freedom, nothing can be done about it. It is called sin because it ultimately resides in corporate human freedom and can be resisted.

This transition from the context of sin as something individually personal to something that is social, participated in by persons but without their direct control, sets up a sphere of ambiguity and a need for language as clear and as challenging as the situation itself. Racism, as social and cultural sin, calls for a new perspective, and the success of this application of the Exercises depends on making it intelligible.

To introduce this constructive interpretation of the Exercises by allowing them to address racism as a system, we turn to an analogy of the recent past to illustrate what is going on. In 1968, at Medellín, the Latin American Bishops Conference, responding to the Second Vatican Council, described broadly the structural social division of the rich and the poor as social sin and expressed their concern for the masses of the poor who were the victims of social injustice. This was something of a departure for a church that dealt with personal sin sacramentally and homiletically rather

------

porate sin," "institutional sin," "sin of the world." In each case it is contrasted with a personal sinful act that implicates individual freedom, responsibility, and thus guilt, that is, personal responsibility for the wrong-doing.

than on the basis of critical analysis of society and questions about its own pastoral practice. Inspired by the Bishops Conference, the Jesuits of Central America at a meeting in 1969 decided to use the Spiritual Exercises in a province retreat to meditate on their spirituality and pastoral practice in the light of the situation, "the reality" in which they were living.[2]

Ignacio Ellacuría played a dynamic role in this initiative. He was part of a team that interpreted the Spiritual Exercises in a way that responded to the concrete context in which team members were living. In 1971 Jon Sobrino interrupted his theological study in Frankfurt and did the Exercises with a group of younger Jesuits led by Ellacuría. Sobrino likened his experience of Ellacuría's approach to the Exercises as an awakening from sleep. The new perspective lay in the shift of attention from "my" sins to the objective situation of sin that surrounded them. "In the *Exercises* we speak of sorrow for my sins, but it was not difficult to feel the immense sorrow and personal suffering of the poor Central Americans, product of the many historical sins."[3]

Ellacuría explained his interpretation of the Spiritual Exercises in a series of eight lectures at the University of Central America in San Salvador in 1974. He used extensive notes for the lectures rather than written texts.[4] In these lecture notes Ellacuría shares in theoretical terms how the Ex-

---

2. Robert Lasalle-Klein recounts these developments in his history of Jesuits in Central America, *Blood and Ink: Ignacio Ellacuría, Jon Sobrino, and the Jesuit Martyrs of the University of Central America* (Maryknoll, NY: Orbis Books, 2014).

3. Jon Sobrino with Charo Mármol, *Theology without Deception: God, the Poor, and Reality in El Salvador* (Maryknoll, NY: Orbis Books, 2023), 39.

4. See n. 1 on p. 1.

ercises have to be interpreted as addressing the social historical context in which they are presented. The more they
draw the actual social conflict of the situation into the interpretation, the more the Exercises will open up existential
meaning. Sobrino describes how this affected him: "Something deep and true was present, something that did not
come from on high and distant, but from below, with its
own authority, not borrowed."[5] Ellacuría was calling for the
Jesuits to resituate the dynamics of the Exercises into the
conditions of the actual society and culture in which they
were living so that the meaning of everything Ignatius suggested became infused with present-day social exigency. Instead of beginning the Exercises with an examination of
one's personal sins, he refocused attention on the social injustice that defined a challenge to Christian existence and
provided the context of Jesuit ministry.

Addressing racism in America as context for the Spiritual
Exercises represents a shift in their interpretation that is analogous to the move of Ellacuría. The new framework influences the whole course of the Exercises, and it begins most
markedly in the first week, which deals with sin. Whereas Ellacuría interpreted the Exercises from the perspective of the
social, historical, and conflictive context of what he called
"the third world" in which the poor were systemically and
unjustly oppressed, the analysis here focuses on the racism
described in the previous chapter. The reference to Ellacuría does not entail exegeting his thought; this is not a
study of Latin American liberation theology. But in a me-
thodical way that is partly similar and partly quite different
from Ellacuría, the present interpretation of the Exercises
changes the focus from an individual personal perspective

---

5. Sobrino, *Theology without Deception*, 39.

on Christian life to a personal but socially attentive perspective on the actual social and cultural situation that deeply influences American life. The term "social" refers to the relationships between people within the nation that are influenced by class, ethnicity, race, economic status, and other identifiers. The term "cultural" refers to the meanings and values that are embedded in the languages and behaviors of groups large and small. The social and cultural dimensions of life together can be observed, described, studied, and objectified. Such social analysis does not restrict consciousness; it expands awareness to a deeper understanding of the actual sphere in which Americans live.

The shift to this social or structural perspective, and implicitly each person's position within it, explains the difficulty one familiar with the Exercises may have in resonating with a social interpretation. On the one hand, it seems to ignore the deep personal relationship with God that each person brings to the Exercises and Ignatius addresses with an examination of conscience. On the other hand, it challenges an embedded social-structural and cultural individualism that undergirds American life. An expansion of horizon and scope of vision to a social perspective requires deliberate attention.

A social and cultural interpretation of the Exercises implies no surrender of a need for a review and attention to personal sin or the other essentials of the Exercises. The shift of focus to the social historical plane does not obliterate but has to appeal to individual personal attention. This constructive interpretation of the Exercises implies no exclusiveness; it does not compete with attention to personal sin but is simply a different approach. It involves interpreting the social context of the spiritual and religious convictions of Christian faith in terms that reflect actual historical life and personal spiritual appropriation. What follows argues for a fuller, more extensive recovery of the meaning of the Spiritual Exercises and the gospel they represent that goes beyond even as it includes personal standing before God as an individual. Recognition of why this transition of focused attention is necessary today provides the premise for the intelligibility of the chapters that follow. It becomes firmer and stronger as it is applied along the way.

According to the structure of the Exercises outlined in Chapter I, the problem the Exercises seek to address is sin. After the discussion of racism, this chapter seeks to show how the transition from an individual's concern for his or her own sin should also be re-appropriated within a framework of a personal concern for structural sin, in this case racism. We begin the analysis by first noting that Ignatius in writing the Exercises was preoccupied with an individual's personal sin. But that focus of attention can be complemented by shifting the framework of the Exercises from the subjectivity of personal sin to an objective account of structural sin. This social perspective entails a larger horizon for human responsibility. Responsibility for one's personal life will be broadened to include concern for a social crisis, indeed, a sinful crisis. People are personally responsible for their personal lives; to what extent are they also responsible to and for the society to which they belong?

Another differentiating factor of the way the Exercises are being interpreted lies in the subject matter of the meditations of the First Week. Ignatius's way of eliciting repentance for sin was meditation on sin. He found the cosmic symbols of sin, as in angels and the first pair of humans, useful. Meditation on the racist dimensions of the history of the United States would play an analogous role for people in America today. But Ignatius focused attention on an intense consideration of the history of each person's personal sin. This introspective meditation, together with an experience of God's forgiveness, released a person's freedom to work for a reform of life in whatever society a person lived. Analogously, recognition of the history of the structural sin of racism transforms the issue and the outcome of spiritual integrity. The social question expands social awareness and responsibility. Meditation on the sins of society provides an occasion to release a personal freedom in the direction of the reform of society itself. Americans need to ask the question about our racist society: "Do we have to live like this?" The question for Christian spirituality in a racist environment relates to how meditation on social injustice motivates an impulse to work for social equality.

In Ignatius's design, the First Week's meditation on sin sets the stage for each person to consider Jesus Christ as the revelation of God's love and God's rule in history. It prepares a person to reorder his or her life toward personal salvation. Appreciation of structural sin, by contrast, includes recognition that personal forgiveness does not deal with the intractability of racism. The Exercises, presented in a social way, open an introverted concern about one's personal sin to look at the structural sin that surrounds everyday behavior. They expand consciousness by revealing social possibilities for a broader range of reactions to society and culture. This defines the theme as we turn to a second look at sin in the First Week of the Exercises, the transition to a social framework and the structural sin of racism, and how meditation on concrete examples of racism would awaken a new level of positive social responsibility.

Sin in the First Week

Early in the text of the Spiritual Exercises, Ignatius defines their purpose (SE, 21). They are meant to gain control of oneself and put order into one's life. He expresses how this end is to be achieved negatively: "without…disordered impulses." A positive reading would imply organizing one's life "on the basis of a decision made in freedom from any disordered attachment."[6] To achieve this, Ignatius organized an intense individual and personal program under guidance. What follows shows the individual character of Ignatius's Exercises to set off the contrast to the perspective raised by structural sin.[7]

Ignatius's statement of purpose directs attention to the condition of the sinner that needs to be overcome. The sinner leads a disordered life; the life of the sinner needs repair; something is wrong. The bondage lies within. The sinner needs to overcome the self, or gain control of his or her life, and reestablish a proper relationship of one's inner ability of self-direction to its proper goal. It needs to become free from attachments that lead one in a wrong direction. That proper direction is defined by this metaphysical "Principle and Foundation": We are created to praise, reverence, and serve God in this life in order to live eternally with God (SE, 23). The way back to freedom involves accurately realizing the full measure of what sin and alienation from God entail. It requires honest self-knowledge. The First Week of the Exercises programs reflection on personal sin in order to initiate the positive goal of enabling a person to overcome the inhibiting bonds of sin and find the freedom

---

6. Michael Ivers, *Understanding the Spiritual Exercises: Text and Commentary, A Handbook for Retreat Directors* (Herefordshire, UK: Gracewing, 1998), 22.

7. It should be noted at the outset that the contrasting perspectives here are "individual" and "social." In both perspectives, the Exercises are always personal, which means intentionally conscious and appropriated. "Individual" does not bear the connotation of "individualist," which suggests a negative myopia. We'll return to this further on.

for a commitment to a way of life that enables the person to move along his or her path of human fulfillment. The means for ordering one's life consists of a life-determining or reforming decision that puts one on track. The whole process relies on God's mercy and grace and is motivated by gratitude and reciprocal love.

The first part of Ignatius's Spiritual Exercises negotiates a deep and extraordinarily extensive set of meditations in order to awaken a thoroughgoing consciousness in the individual of his or her sin. It includes meditations on the pre-historical sin of angels, the originating sin of Adam and Eve, and the sin of an imagined person who for eternity suffers in hell for a single condemning sin. The First Week also includes a method for examining all the sins of one's life. This entails going through one's history recalling the thoughts, words, and actions of a lifetime and considering the degree of their malice (SE, 32–42). Ignatius proposes a meditation on one's history of sinning in which the person making the Exercises remembers and considers the cumulative gravity of those sins. He wants a person to feel deeply within the self the distance sin places between ourselves and the holiness and majesty of God. He asks: "What is all of creation when compared with God? And then, I alone—what can I be?" (SE, 58). "I will look upon myself as a sore and abscess from which have issued such great sins and iniquities and such foul poison" (SE, 58).

Ignatius counsels a somber demeanor during the First Week: "I should not think about pleasant or joyful things" (SE, 78). He encourages a moderate use of penitential practices; one is not to harm oneself, but to discipline the self with physical pain. The externals should reinforce the inner experience of pain, sorrow, and even tears at one's failing.

The point of Ignatius's preoccupation does not lie hidden in the text. It is possible to single out a number of elements that concern him. One is to bring out the terrible consequences of each single sin, and thus its gravity and malice. Personal sin is evil in itself and a personal affront against God. At the same time, reflection opens up the contrast of sin with the holiness of God and with what is expected of human freedom. In the colloquy of "The First Exercise" Ignatius asks the retreatant to imagine Christ on the cross in the act of dying for one's own sins: the horrible effect of sin. And, by contrast, "Reflect on yourself and ask: What have I done for Christ? What am I doing for Christ? What ought I do for Christ?" (SE, 53).

Another motive for this vigorous dwelling on sin is found in the first colloquy of a repetition of the meditations on sin. Ignatius wants a person to know and feel an abhorrence for one's personal sins, to sense deeply the disorder in one's life, in order to stimulate a reaction against it. A person has to become critically aware of the things of this world that lead the self to sin (SE, 63).

Finally, Ignatius encourages a recognition of God's mercy and a feeling of thanksgiving that God has granted the individual person making the Exercises the opportunity and medium of grace in order to change (SE, 61, 71). Ignatius realized that remorse for one's sin intensifies a sense of gratitude for God's mercy. These words do not even begin to match the existential character of the inner dynamic. It can fully fill a person's life with meaning and direction. More simply put, the depth of this personal experience can be life-changing.

This description of the First Week in Ignatius's text shows that its dynamics play out at the deepest part of an individual's spiritual life. The Exercises work within the intimate region of individuals looking at the inner dynamics of their lives, concentrating attention for a time on their infidelities while standing before God. The First Week proposes a quest for honesty about the self within the sight of God. This does not make the Exercises "individualistic," because the personal sins of an individual may be social in character, whether overtly as in fraud or in other actions with immediate social consequences, or implicitly in the sense that all sin in some measure spills over into society. But attention in Ignatius's Exercises is on the responsibility of individuals for their own actions. In this realm, which can sometimes be unfathomable, some sins may be so damaging and life-altering that they cannot be forgiven by victims or oneself, but can only be reached by the Creator God who grounds a moral universe: they require God's mercy for release. The experience of divine mercy then opens up a new dimension of freedom, a new horizon of possibilities, and the dawn of a new life for the individual. Given that dynamic, how do the Exercises work when the focus shifts from personal to structural sin?

Adapting the Exercises to a Structural Framework

In contrast to the intensely individual character of each person's encounter with their own history of sin, the interpretation of the Exercises in response to racism has to do with structural sin. Structural sin relates to an individual's sin by analogy, but major differences distinguish them, and this changes the way the First Week of the Exercises functions. The differences do not alter the structure of the Exercises described in Chapter I; the Exercises still set up a negative situation of sin that is engaged by Christian spirituality. But the character of structural sin elicits subtler demands. This section addresses the shift from a focus on an individual's personal sin to centering the Exercises on structural sin. It describes what is going on here theoretically. The following section specifies the abstract analysis with the case of racism.

The idea of structural sin is hardly new. It appears in Christian tradition in many guises: as a power or force in history in Pauline literature; as an encompassing historical climate due to original sin after Augustine, explicitly in the writing of Walter Rauschenbusch as "the super-personal forces of evil" and "the kingdom of evil";[8] in the idea of institutional sin in Latin American liberation theology; in the realistic descriptions of racism in Black liberation theology. One can begin to define structural sin by a contrast with individual personal sins, which preoccupied Ignatius. Individual sins are injurious acts freely and deliberately performed by an individual agent. Second, a person is responsible and should experience guilt for such sinful acts. Guilt here may or may not involve Freudian psychoanalytic dimensions. More directly, but not less deeply, guilt means assuming responsibility for personal acts of wrongdoing. Sin also disrupts a positive relationship with God, whose intention for creation is transgressed. Third, the moral response to an awareness of one's sins takes the form of repentance and a change in behavior. Moral theologians insert extensive qualification into this simple account of a reflective awareness of sin, but it suffices as a foil to represent structural sin by contrast with, not as an alternative to, personal sin.

"Structural sin," first of all, refers to a social reality as distinct from an individual personal act. It consists of a set of relationships and patterns of behavior that flow from the relationships. In terms of race, Patrick Saint-Jean calls this systemic racism. "It is as pervasive in our society as the air we breathe. For white people, it may be nearly invisible; it is something that they just take for granted. For people of

8. Walter Rauschenbusch, *A Theology of the Social Gospel* (New York: Abingdon Press, 1945), 69–94.

color, [it] is the experience of our daily lives."[9] The idea of a behavior pattern by definition describes the ways people generally act; it is abstract but not fictitious or merely imagined. The relationships and the actions are real.[10] Ignacio Ellacuría describes structural sins straightforwardly in contrast to social grace by their effects. "Some actions kill (divine) life, and some actions give (divine) life; some belong to the kingdom of sin, others to the kingdom of grace. Some social and historical structures objectify the power of sin and serve as vehicles for the power against humanity, against human life; some social and historical structures objectify grace and serve as vehicles for that power in favor of human life."[11] He calls these social entities "structures"; the behaviors can also be called "institutional" or "social," or "systemic." "To think that sin exists only when and insofar as there is personal responsibility is a mistaken and dangerous devaluation of the dominion of sin."[12]

Second, individuals are not responsible in an obvious sense for the existence of structural sin. That kind of sin has a certain objective existence independent of any given individual prior to their exercise of freedom. On a logical level, structural sin relative to the individual looks more like social temptation that seduces; but social pressure actually influences the behavior of individuals. At the same time and some-

---

9. Patrick Saint-Jean, *The Spiritual Work of Racial Justice: A Month of Meditations with Ignatius of Loyola* (Vestal, NY: Anamchara Books, 2021), 39.

10. Daniel K. Finn, "What Is a Sinful Social Structure?" *Theological Studies* 77, no. 11 (2016): 136–64.

11. Ignacio Ellacuría, "The Historicity of Christian Salvation," in *Mysterium Liberationis: Fundamental Concepts of Liberation Theology*, ed. I. Ellacuría and J. Sobrino (Maryknoll, NY: Orbis Books, 1993), 275.

12. Ellacuría, "The Historicity of Christian Salvation," 275.

what paradoxically, when social sins are as prevalent as they can be both culturally and socially, people participate in them whether they know it or not. Since Marx, the influence of culture and social distinction on individual consciousness, beginning with language itself, has become common knowledge. Daily life moves forward in a constant exchange between structural influence and ostensibly autonomous agency.

Third, the moral response to an awareness of one's participation in structural sin widens the field of difference. On the one hand, a person may as an individual freely participate in the structural sin. For example, if the pattern for handling a particular bureaucratic process consists of bribes, one can knowingly do what everyone does because it is the way things work. This becomes an individual sin. On the other hand, even when individuals refuse to pay the bribe, as long as they do not expose it or try to thwart it, they continue to participate in and help sustain the system. Social relationships thus create common bonds of cooperation that make members complicit in group behavior. Social ethicists can describe situations, proffer principles, and parse individual responsibility, but the existential complicity of each actor is much more difficult to establish.[13]

Social structures and how they work solicit the attention of many disciplines: history, sociology, the sociology of knowledge, cognitive science, and, of course, ethics. Social structures evolve with humanity itself. Peter Berger and Thomas Luckmann broadly describe the dynamics. The actions of any society emerge out of human subjectivity and may become the standard way of doing things. Any behavior may become institutionalized and operate as a corporate

---

13. Kenneth R. Himes, "Social Sin and the Role of the Individual," *Annual of the Society of Christian Ethics* 6 (1986): 183–218.

habit. But once behaviors are routinized and the patterns are set, they gain a certain objectivity as the models into which people are socialized. At this stage they may dictate the way things should be done and achieve a certain normative value. Social structures thus possess an intrinsic and somewhat paradoxical tension: They are grounded in contextual human reaction, that is, subjectivity, but they seem endowed with a certain objective authority.[14] This paradox underlies the subtlety of social sin.

Social ethics sets up various ways in which criteria may be applied to determine the character of social structures as sinful and the seriousness of the injury. Ellacuría's formula points in the direction of a holistic value judgment described as a negative experience of contrast. Patricia McAuliffe describes analytically the experience as it is used by Edward Schillebeeckx.[15] It possesses three dimensions. A person or a group experiences a situation as negative, harmful, dehumanizing in a categorical and almost absolute way. This should not be! But such a judgment cannot be experienced or formulated without some kind of perception of the way things should be. Even without any detailed knowledge of this positive background or how to redress the situation, the affront of the negativity presupposes at least a vague alternative. This dialectic also entails a positive urge to change the situation, to right the wrong. The elements describe the formal foundation of a moral experience. This

---

14. Peter L. Berger and Thomas Luckmann, *The Social Construction of Reality: A Treatise in the Sociology of Knowledge* (Garden City, NY: Anchor Books, 1967), 108–36. "Society is a human product. Society is an objective reality. Man is a social product" (136).

15. This is the same experience that LaReine-Marie Mosely describes in "Negative Contrast Experience: An Ignatian Appraisal," *Horizons* 41 (2014): 74–95.

three-dimensional structure, rather than a succession of stages, describes common moral perception prior to ethical argument.[16] Applied to social injustice, it could be called a social categorical imperative.

Once it is recognized, the paradox of structural sin can be described further in the tension between its being both structural and sinful. As a social pattern it is prior to individual freedom; ordinarily, no single person is responsible for it. Yet it exists only as a function of human participation, and all are affected in some measure by common cultural structures of meaning and social practices. Structural sin is social because it exists as routinized human activity, causes injury to social order and life, and should not be; it is sin because it exists only as a function of human freedom and action. The Lisbon earthquake was not a sin, but anti-Semitism and racism are sins. Structural sin hovers between corporate temptation and a second social "nature," in the Thomistic sense of a principle of operation that silently guides human response and has real effects in the individual acts it spawns. Structural sin is not original sin, which is linked to the symbols of Adam and Eve and was not a historical event but a mythic symbol and powerful enough in its own right. But structural sin is an actually constituent part of the fabric of history and involves ever-new cohorts of corporate actors.

---

16. Patricia McAuliffe, *Fundamental Ethics: A Liberationist Approach* (Washington, DC: Georgetown University Press, 1993), 1–38. Johann Baptist Metz writes: "The essential dynamics of history is the [1] memory of suffering as a negative awareness of [2] the freedom that is to come, and [3] as a stimulus to act within the horizon of this history in such a way as to overcome suffering." Johann Baptist Metz, *Faith in History and Society: Toward a Practical Fundamental Theology*, trans. J. Matthew Ashley (New York: Crossroad, 2007), 104. This global view of history places a negative experience of contrast at its dynamic core.

The relevance of this discussion for the Spiritual Exercises becomes operative in the recognition that structural sin is an objective reality and in how one relates to it as an individual social participant. Some people, in so many varying degrees, accommodate their behavior to social sin. "Of course I offer kickbacks in my contracts; that's the way the system operates!" In this case, one yields to social temptation and converts structural sin into an individual personal sinful act with social dimensions. This type of sin fits within the category of individual personal sins reviewed in Ignatius's First Week. With repentance, such sins can be forgiven. Other people may be knowing but reluctant participants in sinful cultural and social patterns of behavior because they cannot imagine ways of escaping them. Still others may not recognize social injustice as such. Warped ideas and disvalues fill the crannies of daily life, from vocabulary to theory, from gesture to decision. Even escape from society appears as dereliction of duty: big and small; inescapable sin on one side, sin of omission on the other.

Here lies the shift in the logic of the Spiritual Exercises when they are directed toward social sin. Ignatius's First Week comes to a first level of closure in recognition of sin and God's forgiveness. This includes radical inner liberation; radical because it affects the roots of human freedom. But one cannot really be liberated from some social sins; they form part of the milieu in which human beings live. When Ignacio Ellacuría asked his fellow Jesuits in the early 1970s to adjust the Spiritual Exercises to the world of systemic suppression of the poor in deadly conflict with Christian values, he was introducing a turn of Ignatian spiritual life from the individual personal sphere of spiritual autonomy to a spiritual life attuned to actual society, especially in its unconscious and mortal mechanisms. It required a conversion of the already converted, a new way of seeing things from a social perspective over which one had much less control. While this is a major shift of focus, it would be a mistake to see these two foci as competing with each other. The social perspective does not eliminate the individual-personal; it expands human life by enlarging its horizon. It connects one more deeply with the actual world, with oneself, and with God.

Racism as Structural Sin

Chapter II offered a brief analysis of racism in the United States with a definition, a history going back to the introduction of slavery in America, racism's structural components, and its dynamics. The centerpiece is white supremacy. The descriptive analytical account of racism can be enhanced by looking at racism in terms of structural sin, recognizing it as a form of objective or institutionalized sin. This designation provides a deeper understanding of racism and clarifies further the subject matter at hand. The description of racism as sin fits it into the framework of the Exercises and opens a way of making racism a subject matter in the meditations and contemplations of the First Week.

The description of racism as structural sin offers a way of underlining the objective character of its existence as distinct from the intentions of this or that individual. An individual action may be racist because it is motivated by racial prejudice. But racism as a system cannot be reduced to the actions of individual persons or groups: it is *structural* and *social* sin; it subsists in and infects social relationships and patterns of behavior whose routinization gives them a semi-autonomous existence relative to individuals. This means that individuals are not responsible for its existence at any particular time or morally responsible in an individual personal sense for its ongoing existence. All Americans are by degrees socialized into or exposed to the cultural and social reality of racism. Its history in America shows in ugly detail the injurious character of its effects in terms of human suffering. It destroys human life.

But the objective system is structural *sin* because it does not exist apart from human behavior. People are not born racist; they learn racist reactions. Within the objective patterns, racism refers to the ways people act consistently. Each person becomes a carrier. Racism principally refers to social and cultural patterns of white action relative to Blacks, even though its effects are more diffuse and include all members of society. The abstract character of this language demands ever deeper analysis in order to critically penetrate both the intractability of the condition and its subjective grounding in order to discover how as a community of subjects we can do better.

The distinction between cultural and social racism may be reiterated here in order to clarify the discussion short of technical social analysis. A cultural understanding of racism asks about the meaning and value of race or races in relation to each other: how do people appropriate race? Cultural aspects of racism reside in the ideas, meanings, and values that are assigned to people on the basis of race. Cultural appreciation refers to the subjective appreciations, the connotations, and the values associated with designation by race. Racism feeds on negative description and devaluation.[17] By contrast, a social understanding of racism describes how

---

17. For example, white culture may explain racism by Black behavior. Recall the finding of sociologist Eduardo Bonilla-Silva cited in the previous chapter: "In the eyes of most Whites, for instance, evidence of racial disparity in income, wealth, education, incarceration, and other matters becomes evidence that there is something wrong with [Blacks] themselves." Bonilla-Silva, *Racism without Racists: Color-Blind Racism and the Persistence of Racial Inequality in America* (New York: Rowman and Littlefield, 2018), 233.

races actually relate to each other; it considers patterns of behavior. The social can be distinguished but not separated from culture by more narrowly focusing on the behaviors that define the relationships between groups. A social understanding of racism examines how, in this case, whites and Blacks relate to each other in a given locale or framework of analysis. The variables are many and always shifting with time, but they are observable and able to be categorized and quantified.

What does it mean to say the United States is infected culturally and socially by the sin of racism? It does not mean that all Americans are racists or that all whites are conscious racists any more than Blacks are consciously racist. It does mean, however, that American culture and society are affected by racist ideas and practices. These ideas, values, actions, and reactions permeate American life and more effectively influence it than most individuals can readily recognize. Racial tensions vary considerably across different fronts. But as a nation Americans are conscious of how race affects the whole of American life, across all the departments of daily decision-making and exchange, with an influence that a Black person cannot afford to ignore, and that no one can escape. The discussion of justice and equality in America cannot bypass a consideration of race. Race designates a major dimension of American life and bears considerable weight in the discussion of a common American morality and spirituality. Precisely as a cultural, structural, and behavioral sin its particular instantiations should become the subject matter for meditation and contemplation.

Meditation on Structural Sin

We have seen how Ignatius put individual personal sin at the center of the First Week of his Spiritual Exercises and surrounded it with the traditional Christian archaeology of sin followed by intense focus on personal sins. Re-centering the Exercises around the phenomenon of structural sin and in particular racism alters the central concern of the First Week of the Exercises. This section discusses practical ways of making this transition from a First Week that deploys the personal sins of individuals to the more objective sphere of structural racism.

Many are the ways of studying and thus representing the various facets of social phenomena. Different ways of presenting the manifestations of racism lie open to the presenter of the Exercises. But two sources offer possibilities for accenting specific aspects of racism and furnish distinctively different spheres for meditation or contemplation. The first turns to historical narratives of overt forms of racial hatred, somewhat less blatant today in the United States than before World War II, but still far from being eradicated; the second represents more indirect, systemic, and less sensational forms of racist activity that continue to punish Blacks.

The first source is found in flagrant acts of violence against Blacks during the period of slavery, after Emancipation, and still present today. It is hard to read, let alone comprehend, Jim Crow when, especially but not exclusively in the South, direct, violent, and dehumanizing action of mobs killed Blacks, intimidated Black communities, and were not held accountable but were sometimes esteemed for it.

An example of meditation on overt racist behavior can be found in James Cone's theological consideration of the act of lynching in *The Cross and the Lynching Tree*.[18] In the first

---

18. James Cone, *The Cross and the Lynching Tree* (Maryknoll, NY: Orbis Books, 2011).

chapter Cone describes the experience of Black communities where lynching took place.

> The lynching tree was the most horrifying symbol of white supremacy in black life. It was a shameful and painful way to die. The fear of lynching was so deep and widespread that most blacks were too scared even to talk publicly about it. When they heard of a person being lynched in their vicinity, they often ran home, pulled down shades, and turned out lights—hoping the terror moment would pass without taking the lives of their relatives and friends.[19]

Often a lynching was a public event; it became a way of terrorizing Blacks and exercising white supremacy in a thoroughgoing social way. In other words, it affected the whole Black community and cannot be reduced to individual incidents of hatred and occasional acts of repression. Each lynching was a particular story; but whether the particular victim was guilty or innocent of the offense, the punishment was also inflicted on the community.[20] The frequency of lynchings, the territorial expanse of their occurrence, and the particular barbarity of the practice make their narratives graphic icons of human depravity. Compared with these narratives, meditations on the fall of Adam and Eve appear cerebral and tame.

---

19. Cone, *The Cross and the Lynching Tree*, 15.

20. "We cannot forget the terror of the lynching tree no matter how hard we try. It is buried deep in the living memory and psychology of the black experience in America. We can go to churches and celebrate our religious heritage, but the tragic memory of the black holocaust in America's history is still waiting to find theological meaning." Cone, *The Cross and the Lynching Tree*, 159–60.

A second source for meditations on socially mediated racist systems is found in various systemic social practices that Black people consistently encounter but not as dramatic public events. They occur in plain sight, yet have become so routine that they may be ignored as systems that target Blacks. Without limiting sinful social situations to these, prominent examples are found in the areas of policing, work, religion, healthcare, housing, education, and recreation. Most people are aware of prejudice in these areas, but few outside of those who experience it know the comprehensive range, the systemic character, or the extent of the damage that is done to individuals and to a large percentage of the community at large.[21] In some areas, the laws surrounding the practices actually promote the repressive practices, sometimes by virtue of unintended consequences, at other times intentionally.[22] The variety of cases shows that these practices cannot be explained satisfactorily by the motives governing each event; they constitute social patterns of behavior that are sometimes supported by deficient regulation, or allowed to go unaddressed, or actively promoted. The cases also provide the way into the subject matter by contemplation.

Various events also provide subject matter that transcends the particular and teach principle by dramatic illustration. For example, in the area of policing, the murder of

---

21. Conor M. Kelly, a moral theologian, gives a straightforward account of how systemic practices targeting Blacks in these areas form a stable part of American social life. See *Racism and Structural Sin: Confronting Injustice with the Eyes of Faith* (Collegeville, MN: Liturgical Press, 2023), 57–77. This work is a schematic outline. A fuller analysis of the range of racist activity can be found under "racism" in each of the areas just enumerated in any university library.

22. For example, because change is effected through the election of public officials, the best way of preventing change is by restricting the right to vote or neutralizing it.

George Floyd in broad daylight on a city street and surrounded by witnesses, among them other police officers and a person filming the event, has become an icon for racially motivated policing. This incident has in fact been appropriated by a large number of Americans with deeply disorienting effect. It was a national negative experience of contrast. It continues to raise a string of fundamental questions that grow more disturbing by their failure to produce answers or to even generate a common will to find a way forward.

Another discriminating social activity is red-lining that inhibits loans to Blacks because of the risks involved in lending to those who live in impoverished areas. "They literally drew red lines on the maps to mark off the neighborhoods with more people of color, discouraging banks from loaning to homebuyers in those areas."[23] The practice has snowballing effects that disable poor communities generally and Black neighborhoods in particular. A social imagination can read the effects on everyday life that has been cut off from the ordinary mechanisms of economic advancement. Questions of housing and neighborhood affect education because of the way schools are financed; deficient education affects motivation and opportunity of employment and earning, which affect insurance and healthcare, and the ability to raise children who can compete in society.[24] Case study and narrative provide subject matter for contemplation that observes

---

23. Kelly, *Racism and Structural Sin*, 64.

24. For a dramatic contrast in the goals of city planning, compare the often racist motivation of Robert Moses in Robert A. Caro, *The Power Broker: Robert Moses and the Fall of New York* (New York: Vintage Books, 1975), and the community-building ideas of neighborhood planning of Mindy Thompson Fullilove, *Urban Alchemy: Restoring Joy in America's Sorted-Out Cities* (New York: New Village Press, 2013).

and internalizes the structural sin that is perpetrated by agents who are analogously the equivalents of members of a lynch mob even though the action takes place in bureaucratic offices through computer screens.

As a general rule, meditation on present-day cases of racism does not seek to stir a sense of personal guilt for situations that are beyond individuals' ability to remedy. On the contrary, it aims at penetrating below the surface of statistics and appearance and exposing unjust social mechanisms. It aims at mediating a negative experience of contrast at overt and hidden injustice and the diminishment of human life. There are no charges brought against white privilege or Black favoritism, but there is a common appeal to recognize injustice that generates a common human imperative: This should not stand. At this exact juncture the profundity of Martin Luther King Jr. rises to the surface; the beloved community is common cause. We Americans shall overcome. We cannot be neutralized by partisanship.

The Logic of the First Week

Contemplation or meditation on structural sin does not yield the same reactions as do reflections on individual personal sins. The accent of what one is looking for in the meditations on sin shifts with the kind of sin that is being considered. It is possible, of course, that the one making the Exercises is an overt racist who acts aggressively against Black people. But knowing or unknowing participation in subtler or even concealed systemic racist activity changes the question to one more properly framed in terms of cultural and social awareness. The issue is less accusatory and, like the situation itself, more objective than the overt terms of personal responsibility. For example, one might ask: "Am

I aware of the extent to which racial differentiation affects the dynamics of American culture and society and the harm it causes?" "What is my place in a society whose dynamics are so overtly guided by race?" "What is my participative role in the structural systems of racism?" "Can I in any measure resist patterns of racism that operate in my environment?" These are existential questions, but they can be addressed objectively. They do not necessarily divide people, because they apply to all members of a society. People can use "we" language here. The issues can be treated noncompetitively, as in an AA meeting, because there are no secret answers that others cannot appreciate and learn from. In other words, the questions can be addressed across racial boundaries, and shared responses might be helpful to all.

The issues of how to recognize and how to respond to social sin need more reflection. Shifting the attention of the First Week to social sin requires that the aim of the meditation, what Ignatius called the desired outcome, be accurately formulated. On the one hand, meditation on social sin differs from looking at personal sin and responsibility. Although one consciously participates in social patterns of behavior, such behavior can be spontaneous and unknowing relative to their effects. From the perspective of responsibility, which is intrinsic to the notion of sin, the nature of structural sin differs greatly from the individual's personal intent of wrong-doing in Ignatius's First Week. The first goal in the examination of structural sin veers toward expansion of consciousness of one's social and cultural context. It aims at an internal recognition of the dynamics of structural sin and one's social participation in society as a member. Contemplation or meditation seeks to insert the one making the Exercises into the actual dynamics of the culture and society in which they live. The First Week aims at reflective self-knowledge and acknowledgment that one participates in society, that it has shaped one's behavior, and that one is not merely a passive participant but one with a role as a member of the community. With regard to racism, for example, a person might ask, what is the racial character of society, and where is one positioned in the sphere of race relationships?

On the other hand, these objective questions implicitly include the consideration of what each person contributes to society. Participation in culture and society should be conscious, reflective, intentional, and thus also personal. Consideration of the social sin of racism places the self within a tension between "I cannot do anything" to change a social situation and "I must do something" because I am part of the community. This tension defines the nature of social existence. Structural sin and a negative contrast experience of it create a certain pressure toward a possible redirection of one's style of life. It is accompanied by a shift away from personal responsibility *for* the situation, in the sense of involving individual guilt, toward a responsibility *within* and *to* the situation of one's own society, all of its people, and its common good. This amounts to a call of the common good to the self, a summons to responsible citizenship, an appeal beyond the dialectic of personal guilt–forgiveness–gratitude to explicit forms of gratitude-in-action and a socially active spirituality that requires thought about what one can do.

H. Richard Niebuhr conceived of the responsible and responding self as the clearinghouse of ethics and spirituality.[25] Human beings define themselves by their responding to the actions that shape them: the forces of nature, other

---

25. H. Richard Niebuhr, *The Responsible Self: An Essay in Christian Moral Philosophy* (New York: Harper & Row, 1978).

selves, the past, and God in the action of positing and sustaining their own existence. Spirituality always moves forward. It can move beyond the past. Persons continually
refine their spiritualities by how they respond in the present
to the world of nature and their communities. They face an
expanding accountability to the society that surrounds
them, to the world, to the one human family, and to God as
their grounding Presence. This provides a context for attending to and learning from the negative history and sociology of racism. In them one may discern a social project
that will address the issue, and to which one can dedicate
the self as to a cause that is also God's cause.

This logic shifts the emphasis of the First Week from a
sense of guilt and shame drawn from meditation on the negativity of personal sin and the history of our individual failure to respond to the question "What have I done for
Christ?" It introduces another question on the level of a divided society striving to become a community. The new emphasis recognizes the character of the issue of race and
refuses to hide behind its objectivity. Social responsibility is
also personal; it engages human freedom. But the more
comprehensive intention of the First Week becomes aimed
at the third Christian question asked by Ignatius: "What
ought I do for Christ?" (SE, 53). This challenge of the future
does not imply that the sense of malice and the gravity of
personal sin that Ignatius so deeply felt will be lost or
negated; that may be taken for granted as one entertains a
new focus of attention. The gravity and malice of sin re-
appear in the ravages of racism and its history. This involves a different kind of appeal to conscientiousness
beyond a recognition of personal sin. Meditations on examples of racism open up a consciousness of consistent aggression against groups of people. It stretches the self to a

social consciousness of society as a perpetrator, of oneself as a member of society, and of a responsibility for society that creates an inner ontic desire to cooperate in negating the repression of human life. The meditation on structural sin turns positive when it elicits a desire for change that is congruent with the rule of God.

To sum up here, the change from an individual's perspective to a social perspective on sin requires a reorientation of language. The difference appears in the contrast between individual and collective knowledge and action. The subject matter here is not personal sin but structural sin. This offers participants in the Exercises a new way of understanding their relationship with God through their being involved in their social context. But just how does one's being part of a racist society affect one's relationship with God? Christopher Pramuk explores the role of God in the discussion of radical social injustice such as anti-Semitism and racism and invokes the testimony of Abraham Joshua Heschel and Frederick Douglass.[26] From one perspective, the relationship to God does not change the configurations of history. But God as Presence digs down into anthropology and interrupts the conversation about society with transcendent depth, honesty, and a call to responsibility. The two dimensions of all personal existence, everyone's relationship with God and with society in terms of social justice, supply different planes of response. They do not necessarily imply each other on the level of conscious awareness because people can compartmentalize and not make the connection. Consequently, one has to pay close attention to the issue of reception when speaking of responsibility for the structural

---

26. Christopher Pramuk, "The Question of God in the Struggle for Racial Justice," *Horizons* 48, no. 1 (2021), 172–94.

sin of racism. The sin of omission is where the conversation becomes delicate. One can accuse oneself of sin but not another person. But all can discuss together social conditions.

More pointedly, Pramuk makes a case for not abandoning a goal of communicating a subjective sense of personal shame and confusion (Ignatius) accompanying a consideration of objective social injustice (Sobrino). He asks the question: "To what extent are such interior exercises in (white) self-examination . . . actually helpful for (Black) living, much less for the dead? In short, is shame the best vehicle for the personal and cultural metanoia we desire to see?"[27] He finds positive responses to the question in recent German and Jewish experience through Gregory Baum and Abraham Joshua Heschel, respectively. From Baum he learns the idea of "guilt by common heritage" as distinct from personal guilt. "Without grieving over the past . . . people cannot come to a truthful understanding of the present nor adopt a responsible orientation to the future."[28] And from Heschel he borrows the idea of social responsibility: "Some are guilty; all are responsible."[29] These reflections accurately describe how people may receive and be moved by meditation on and contemplation of the many histories and events of racism.

---

27. Christopher Pramuk, "The Gift of Tears: White Metanoia at the Foot of the Black Cross," in *Praying for Freedom: Racism and Ignatian Spirituality in America*, ed. Laurie Cassidy (Collegeville, MN: Liturgical Press, 2024), 119.

28. Gregory Baum, *Essays in Critical Theology* (Kansas City: Sheed & Ward, 1994), 199–200, as cited by Pramuk in "The Gift of Tears," 121.

29. Abraham Joshua Heschel, *Moral Grandeur and Spiritual Audacity: Essays*, ed. Susannah Heschel (New York: Farrar, Straus and Giroux, 1996), 231, as cited in Pramuk, "The Gift of Tears," 122.

But in the presentation of the Exercises one has to be very cautious about an implied accusation of personal sin. The reason why personal sin is the prime analogate for the very notion of sin lies in its connection with knowledge, freedom, and responsibility. This more readily appears in considerations of personal sin than in considerations of structural sin. There is no sin without responsibility. At the same time, thinking of responsibility exclusively in terms of an individual's freedom has created a major obstacle to the effectiveness of Christian preaching about structural injustice.

There is a better way of presenting responsibility for structural sin that actually penetrates more deeply into consciousness because of its objectivity. It appears in Ta-Nehisi Coates's presentation of the case for Black reparations.[30] The sensibility of justice is found in an analogy drawn from inheritance. One cannot inherit the fortune of one's family without assuming responsibility for the debts. It was expressed by the president of Yale University in 1810: "We inherit our ample patrimony with all its encumbrances; and are bound to pay the debts of our ancestors."[31] This does not respond to all the questions that reparations elicit: Who pays? To whom? How much? How distributed? All of these would have to be worked out. But the logic represents sound justice, and it can be entertained deeply in a way that transcends subjective guilt and engages a constructive social responsibility for the future.

The burden of this chapter lies in a recognition that a shift in the conception of the sin that the Spiritual Exercises addresses represents a fairly comprehensive reorganization

---

30. Ta-Nehisi Coates, "The Case for Reparations," *The Atlantic Monthly* (June 2014), 54–71.

31. Cited by Coates in "The Case for Reparations," 65.

of the language used by Ignatius. It involves more subtle adjustments than the shift of a melody to a new key. Structural sin is analogously sin, but very different from an individual's personal sin. It arises out of consideration and internalization of one's environment and requires carefully crafted new language because it makes new demands on personal freedom. It challenges people to envisage a new reality, a common good, and urges participation in the project.

In the Christian tradition of faith, the struggle with sin is intimately connected with Jesus of Nazareth. He proffers God's forgiveness, but more importantly at this juncture of the discussion, a model for human existence. The next chapter will explore Jesus's ministry as a source of ideals for constructive human living in the context of racism.

IV

The Meaning of Jesus
in a Racist Situation

At the end of the First Week of Ignatius's Spiritual Exercises, the individual dealing with personal sins reaches some measure of closure in self-knowledge, repentance, and the recognition of God's mercy and forgiveness. This provides a spiritual platform for further probing into the question: "What ought I do for Christ?" The emphasis on the structural sin of racism requires some adjustments in these dynamics. Little in the cultural and social situation of racism changes with the conversion of an individual. Racism, hidden in the metaphors of ordinary speech and the exchanges of everyday behavior, continues to pervade and infect social life. Actions carry it; responses reveal it. Nevertheless, a consideration of the ministry of Jesus, when placed in the context of racism, can and should influence a Christian's basic attitude toward the situation. The average American lives on one of the two sides of Black and white, some more intensely than others. After considering racism during the First Week of the Exercises, a person looks to Jesus of

Nazareth for a way to live in this situation before the face of God as represented by him. One might say that Ignatius spontaneously followed the intrinsic logic of Christian faith in looking at Jesus as a mediator of God in response to human sin.[1]

Ignatius introduces the Second Week of the Spiritual Exercises with an exercise titled "The Kingdom of Jesus Christ." It serves as a formal bridge from a focus on sin to its antidote in the mediation of God by Jesus of Nazareth. This chapter begins with a consideration of how Ignatius leads a person into the series of contemplations on the ministry of Jesus of Nazareth and the rule of God that is found there.

One can consider Jesus in the Second Week of the Spiritual Exercises on two distinct levels. This chapter begins a first reflection on Jesus in more objective terms; the following chapter continues the discussion on a more subjective level, that of the disciple.[2] Both chapters take up the stories of Jesus in the New Testament and interpret their content in

---

1. Jon Sobrino explains: Ignatius takes the negative side of existence seriously: evil, injustice, sin, and death. But the Spiritual Exercises go beyond sin being forgiven to its being undone. "Strictly speaking, he wants sin to be eradicated," whether it be lodged in the person or in the world. "Spirituality does not come down to 'good intentions' or the 'purity' of one's intentions. Ignatian spirituality comes down to fleshing out one's inner intentions in history even as Jesus of Nazareth did. Expressed in negative terms, it comes down to eradicating sin." The response to sin, then, is found in the Second Week, in Jesus's active ministry against the effects of sin in the world. Jon Sobrino, "The Christ of the Spiritual Exercises," in *Christology at the Crossroads: A Latin American Approach* (Maryknoll, NY: Orbis Books, 1978), 403–4.

2. This is not a hard distinction; each can involve the other. The finer point concerns the election or life-decision that emerges out of these considerations of Jesus's ministry. This is discussed in the following chapter.

light of racism. This chapter examines the meaning of Jesus's representation of the rule of God in his ministry as portrayed in the gospels. The engagement with Jesus through exemplary passages pales in comparison with the four gospels themselves, but the chosen texts set a direction for contemplations that probe more deeply. The gospel passages presented in this chapter illustrate important qualities of a fuller program. In Chapter V the question of appropriation, "What am I to do?" steers the meditations and contemplations in the direction of decision-making.

A number of basic factors supply a map for the present chapter: the selection of the topics, the stories, and the way they are presented. The gospel texts are chosen to point to a way in which the stories of Jesus might contribute to a response to racism. The idea that Jesus offers a distinctive revelation of God reflects the foundation of Christian spirituality and of Christianity itself. The world to which Jesus represents God is sinful, and in this case, the form of sin is structural. Jesus reveals through the words and actions of his ministry an appropriate response to racism. Sometimes theology seems content with a theological analysis of his person constituted by two natures, human and divine. But that conception too depends on appropriation of Jesus actively revealing God by his ministry. Part of the genius of Ignatius's Exercises consists in their bringing people back to the original dynamics of Jesus mediating an existential encounter with God. Jesus is a parable of God. He mediates God narratively by his words and actions strung together in his ministry. In so doing, he also acts out God's intentions for the way human beings should live.

The Spiritual Exercises fix on the conviction that Jesus reveals a God who stands opposed to sin. It is not clear whether Jesus was more concerned with structural sin or in-dividual sin.[3] The structural dimension of sin may not be no-ticed by an individual reader of the gospel; it escapes general notice in the piety of an individualist culture and so-ciety. Highlighting racism as a framework for doing the Ex-ercises brings this aspect of Jesus's teaching forward. It broadens the horizon of the program of the Spiritual Exer-cises and expands the consciousness and the conscience of those who make them.

The discussion presupposes that God acts in history through human agents, perhaps even unknowing agents like Cyrus II of Persia (Isa 45:1–7). The person of Jesus demonstrates the principle for Christian consciousness. The idea of history refers to the world, the series of events across time, and the human subjectivity that both participates in and experiences the phenomena. History is temporal reality mixed with reaction to it, sometimes recorded but far from adequately. God does not act in history as a creature, but as Creator and sustainer. People talk about the will and inten-tion of God, but these are carried forward in human history through human agents rather than by God as an intervening actor. Modernity has an accentuated consciousness of this non-intervening Presence, and Ignacio Ellacuría's idea of historicization integrates this element of modernity into Ig-natius's Christian spirituality.

The idea of spirituality underlying this project was de-fined earlier, but it will not be out of place to underline again its narrative character. A case can be made that both the

---

3. This ambiguity becomes apparent in some of the parables of Jesus: he often appears more concerned about and focused on the be-havior of the community, Israel, than the actions of individuals.

gospels and the Spiritual Exercises agree on a broad conception of Christian spirituality as "following Jesus." Although the expansiveness of the phrase begs several questions, it offers some positive emphases that are operative in this chapter. Spirituality is active rather than passive; it consists of responding to God; meditation itself is activity with its own value but also aimed at future behavior. Spirituality tends toward being expansive, inclusive, and comprehensive. It applies to the whole of a person's intentional life rather than a compartment of it. It postulates that, in the following of Jesus, the full range of his reported activity has spiritual value for the follower to the extent that his relationship with God embraces the whole of his individual life.

A last point comes from biblical scholars who study how the gospels portray Jesus of Nazareth. In examining how Jesus appeared to his contemporaries, that is, the prevalent role he adopted and the way he was perceived, three distinct but inseparable categories help in describing his ministry. He was a Jewish teacher; whether he had credentials as a rabbi or not, he was an itinerant religious, moral, and spiritual teacher. He is also portrayed as a prophet, one who announces the views of God on current affairs and thus often appears critical of situations and ways of doing things, sometimes pinpointing specific groups of people. The present-day title of social critic would characterize Jesus fairly accurately. Such persons stimulate conflict and create enemies, and such reactions help explain how he came to be executed. Still other scholars center their interpretation of Jesus around his exorcisms and wonderful healings. The so-called miracle stories taken together refer to something historical in Jesus's ministry, but it is hard to reconstruct what happened in any explanatory way. They represent Jesus attending to physical and spiritual needs. All three functions and roles—teacher, prophet, healer—apply to Jesus as he appears in the gospels, the main source of what we know about him. They account for three of the focusing categories of this chapter.[4]

These principles roughly outline the development of this chapter. It begins with the set-up notion of discipleship; Jesus is presented as one to be followed. It moves to the notion of "the rule of God" which provides a center of gravity that encapsulates the message of Jesus of Nazareth. It then proposes to show how the Exercises represent the gospel portrait of Jesus, not by the affirmations of dogmatics, but performatively in the way he revealed God to people of his day as a teacher, prophet, and healer. The reflection explicitly includes interpretation of how Jesus mediates a Christian response to racism today.

Jesus Christ as Leader

> "My will is to conquer the whole world and all my enemies and thus to enter into the glory of my Father. Therefore, whoever wishes to come with me must labor with me, so that through following me in the pain he or she may follow me also in the glory." (SE, 95)[5]

---

4. Many texts could be chosen to represent Jesus as teacher, prophet, and healer. The chosen texts are not necessarily the best illustrations of the categories. They are chosen somewhat arbitrarily for what they yield. Other stories could easily be substituted to emphasize other aspects of Jesus's ministry within and beyond the three categories.

5. These citations are short clips meant to represent a longer text or gospel story.

To represent the Christian response to sin, Ignatius turned to the sources he had at hand. Originally, this was not a catechism but a life of Christ. It consisted of a compendium of gospel texts, historical commentary reaching back into the patristic period, and prayers. Ignatius also reflected his own past by composing an exercise that consists of a comparison of Jesus with an ideal Christian king chosen by God to accomplish God's will on earth. Should a king like that reach out, no one could resist the call to such service. A fortiori, all should be attracted to Jesus, the divine King (SE, 91–98). This exercise, like a second principle and foundation, sets up the course of the next three weeks of exercises. Rather than exegete the text, a brief commentary re-appropriates the logic of the exercise for an interpretation of Jesus relative to structural racism.[6]

By following the intrinsic logic of Christian faith itself in turning to Jesus as revealer of God, Ignatius also found God's response to the structural sin of racism. Jesus may be characterized as God's representative for Christian faith. In the deep sacramental sense of not only pointing to but also rendering present, Jesus is symbol of God, the condensed event in history through which Christians find God present and self-communicating.

By using gospel texts rather than doctrinal formulas, Ignatius appeals to Jesus's ministry to capture his person and what he mediates. The gospel narrative includes various facets of Jesus's active ministry and the ways he appeals to

---

6. For a close commentary on Ignatius's text, see Michael Ivens, *Understanding the Spiritual Exercises* (Herefordshire, UK: Gracewing; Surrey, UK: Inigo Enterprises, 1998), 77–86. I offer a brief commentary on this exercise in Roger Haight, *Christian Spirituality for Seekers* (Maryknoll, NY: Orbis Books, 2012), 150–55.

people: his teachings in aphorism and parable, his critical commentary on his own faith tradition and its leaders, his exorcisms, and his modeling of Jewish life in actions and events. In other words, Ignatius depicts Jesus as an actor in history, a doer, and he does this in the narrative form of the gospels rather than a description of his person. Ignatius captures the original dynamic way doctrines about Jesus arose out of encounter with his actions in contrast to thinking of what Jesus did on the basis of his status as later formulated by doctrine.

The depiction of Jesus as a king may be best explained in Ignatius's case by his background of royal service. A king or queen represented for him the highest example of a leader who elicited something close to absolute loyalty and service. Reaching back into the medieval period, considering how leadership of a nation and its people as well as responsibility for the common good were understood, and recalling Ignatius's own formation and dedication, one can find the wellspring of the kingly metaphor for Jesus in the Exercises. Whether through a broad process of secularization or the emergence of confidence in scientific explanations of things, we live in a world that rejoices in or suffers from disenchantment; appreciation begins and frequently ends on the pragmatic surface of society. We do not read royalty as sacred. But leadership and charismatic authority still excite the imagination, and the religious authority of Jesus as spiritual leader inspires the lives of hundreds of millions of people.

As a spiritual leader Jesus today is not merely revered but also followed; within the Christian faith tradition Jesus actively mediates God, reveals the character of human existence as standing before a loving Creator God, and sets up standards for human being and living. Ironically, in our own modern period, this reaction to Jesus has taken on a transcultural import as never before. Christianity, exported at first through colonialism, continues to take on meaning that reflects many cultures in differing indigenous ways.

A present-day appreciation of Jesus in a Western democratic setting will probably not be impressed with Ignatius's militarism. A post-colonial reaction spontaneously resists imagery reminiscent of the Crusades. Moderns who turn to the text of the Exercises may be positively offended by Ignatius's language of conquering the world. Theologians actively try to re-appropriate Jesus in an intrinsically pluralistic world. That effort can be enabled by reformulating the mission of the Christian church in terms of human flourishing and reconciliation, not only with God, but with each other as persons and in relation to other faith traditions. This does not completely run across the grain of the Exercises; certain dimensions of Ignatius's spirituality provide clues for a theological method that can addresses these issues.[7]

Where does an appropriation of this exercise leave the discussion? There is no reason why people today cannot appreciate the personal and broader historical situation of any given text and, if it has classical characteristics, re-appropriate them into a historically new and different context. Ignatius has captured from the gospels the original, dynamic, narrative character of Jesus's mediation of God's presence within history. He gives life to phrases like "the will of God" as meaning the flourishing of human existence in community, and Christian spirituality as "being a disciple" or a

---

7. Christophe Theobald draws from the Exercises the principle that "the locus of God's self-revelation is God's living and working in the diversity of *everything* and *every* person" (SE, 235–36). "An Ignatian Way of Doing Theology," *The Way* 43, no. 4 (October 2004): 152. According to Theobald, this principle implicitly acknowledges the pluralism of God's presence, while the election postulates God at work in a unique way in each individual person.

follower of Jesus. Moreover, the vestigial enthusiasm of the royal servant communicates a level of commitment to a cause that can be absolute. The object of that cause is the rule of God.

Jesus and the Rule of God

"This is how you are to pray:
Our Father in heaven, hallowed be your name,
your kingdom come, your will be done,
on earth as in heaven." (Matt 6: 9–10)

The idea of the rule of God plays an important role in Jesus's ministry and thus serves as a point of entry into the way people today might draw spiritual energy in response to racism. As noted earlier, many use the phrase "the rule of God" instead of "the kingdom of God" because it more dynamically represents the Greek expression it translates. Both translate βασιλεία του θεού accurately, but "kingdom" slants the meaning more objectively toward a territory or to an institutional sphere to which God relates with authority and power. The king administers the kingdom. By contrast, the "reign" or "rule" of a ruler shifts attention toward the action of exercising authority and administration. The term spontaneously suggests the subjective act of ruling, the oversight and care of the king. Use of the phrase "the rule of God" stands for the dynamic relationship of God to creatures; it draws scriptural use into the here and now with the help of a theology of creation that understands God as actively present to and sustaining all reality all the time, as well as God's care and concern for what God creates.

The many uses of the language of the rule of God in the gospels show its many distinct qualities. Jesus points to the rule of God as something already present or imminent and also as a future eschatological reality. One can become a part of it now, or it is up ahead, or God's rule is both of these simultaneously. The rule of God is otherworldly or a quality of the temporal order. Jesus gave personalist resonance to the rule of God when he said it "is within you" (Luke 17:21); but the phrase more naturally leans toward something broad, embracive, and social that can be personally appropriated. Even its deeper archaeological roots are ambiguous: Does it draw from the model of the ideal king reflecting God's care for all, or more directly from God as sovereign lawgiver and source of Torah? Rather than confuse things, these many aspects show the depth, power, and versatility of the metaphor. God is God, related to all reality, and as personal Creator loves creation and transmits a sense of purpose for it.

A more specific understanding of the meaning of the rule of God in the ministry of Jesus appeals to the phrasing of the Lord's Prayer (Matt 6:9–13). When Jesus taught his followers to say, "Your kingdom come, your will be done on earth," this seems like a pointed description of the rule of God. If the second phrase, "your will be done on earth," is appositional in relation to God's kingdom coming, it focuses, but does not restrict, the meaning of the rule of God on God's will for creation. This does not mean a controlling will of God that determines each personal situation in defining detail; many situations show that to be too great a paradox to bear. But God's creating power and presence provide a reason that guarantees the value of each person and thus condemns deliberate abuse of persons or any part of creation. The rule of God expresses the concerned intention of the Creator for the integrity of creation generally and in its particulars.

When the rule of God is taken as the basic content of the whole of Jesus's ministry, it transfers to his actions extensive meaning and relevance. It also directs the full weight of God's will against the sin of racism. Whether the rule of God captures a "center" or holistic image that underlies the whole of Jesus's ministry or expresses an encompassing horizon of application, or an underlying conviction and motivating force driving his ministry, it communicates directly to the disciple, one who would follow. The abstract character of the idea coupled with the realism of the stories of Jesus's ministry are in a way replicated in the contemplative exercises. When the rule of God becomes internalized as a metaphor that carries a set of values, it functions like a virtue or a fundamental moral attitude that determines the basic orientation or disposition of a person.[8] Like a reverence for the intrinsic objective value of different forms of being or the recognition of the unique value of each human person, it guides one's responses to the world. This characterization of how the rule of God operated in Jesus's life opens the way to recognizing how one can find light in the stories of his ministry.

This leads to the more direct question of how the ministry of Jesus can help in the formation of a reaction against the racism of our time. The dynamics of how this works begin with noting how Jesus appropriated his own tradition as a model of how Christians might appropriate their own. He did not write a dissertation about God's rule in the Jewish prophets, kings, and psalmists. But he internalized past

---

8. A fundamental moral attitude consists of a habitual or ingrained response to basic moral values as found in something true, good, or beautiful. See Dietrich von Hildebrand, *Fundamental Moral Values* (New York: Books for Libraries Press, 1969).

language and applied it to his present situation. Luke portrays Jesus borrowing the language of Isaiah and using it to describe the possibilities of his own message in his own time. Isaiah spoke of sight to the blind and the lame walking. Jesus said to the people of Nazareth: "Today this scripture passage is fulfilled in your hearing" (Luke 4:21). In an analogous way, looking back to Jesus from the perspective of a racist situation, Jesus surely does not positively describe policies and laws for twenty-first-century America. But he does communicate the perspective of the rule of God. He communicates fundamental moral attitudes toward the world and the present culture, and against the profound injustice that characterizes American society. He communicated these basic dispositions less in propositional formulas and more forcefully through his ministerial behavior: his prophetic criticism and his symbolic actions.

An approach to the meaning of the rule of God in present-day culture and society can be developed on the premise of Paul when he wrote to the Philippians that they should take on the basic attitudes that can be harvested from the ministry of Jesus (Phil 2:5). He proceeded to illustrate that with a hymn to the humility and exaltation of Jesus. But the invitation to "put on" the virtues of Jesus virtually describes the birth of Christianity and its inner logic. Christianity itself emerged out of discipleship. On that premise, the question becomes specific. What does the rule of God mean in the face of structural racism and the recognition that it is wrong, sinful, and should not be?[9] It entails taking stock of society, recognizing the injustice, and assessing its moral gravity. It includes acknowledgment that one participates in society and bears the weight of the situation. Reflection on the

---

9. See the negative experience of contrast described in the preface and Chapter III.

moral situation leads to analogical reflection that sees structural patterns underlying the dynamics of racism in America, caste in India, and the treatment of Jews in Nazi Germany.[10] The meaning of the rule of God had variations in Jesus's time and in his own usage. But the common contrastive idea of the rule of God, diametrically opposed to structural sin, can inspire any human being to higher ideals.

Jesus as Teacher

> There was a rich man who dressed in purple garments and fine linen and dined sumptuously each day. And lying at his door was a poor man named Lazarus, covered with sores, who would gladly have eaten his fill of the scraps that fell from the rich man's table.... When the poor man died, he was carried away by angels to the bosom of Abraham. The rich man also died and was buried, and from the netherworld, where he was in torment, he raised his eyes and saw Abraham far off and Lazarus at his side. (Luke 16:19–23)

Jesus was an itinerant teacher; he went to a town or village, taught in the synagogue, healed those who came to him, and then moved on. Some draw portraits of Jesus likening him to a Jewish version of a Greek cynic philosopher who had disciples and went from place to place teaching about how

---

10. See Isabel Wilkerson, *Caste: The Origins of Our Discontent* (New York: Random House, 2020), passim. The point does not lie in their different geneses and dynamics, but in their analogous structures that illuminate each other. So too, by contrast, various dimensions of the rule of God elicit deeper appreciation of the negative effects of racism.

to live authentically.[11] Jesus taught with moral and spiritual discourses, parables, allegories, and memorable sayings. The example of the parable of the Rich Man and Lazarus has an overt message similar to Luke's version of the Beatitudes: "Blessed are you who are poor, for the kingdom of God is yours"; "But woe to you who are rich, for you have received your consolation" (Luke 6:20, 24). This means that the world exists within the rule of God and has justice at its foundation. The human community itself supplies no such moral foundation. Today, the follower of Jesus says that, as unimaginably large as it is, we live in a moral universe; in the sustaining power of the living God, it is not dead to right and wrong. Jesus the teacher, situated within Jewish tradition, shed the light of the rule of God on the situation of human existence in the world.

Jesus taught by preaching and acting. The Gospel of Mark describes a day in Jesus's ministry: it took place in Capernaum. On the morning of a Sabbath, Jesus stood and taught in the synagogue; afterward he entered the house of Simon and Andrew where he healed Simon's feverish mother-in-law; in the afternoon after sunset he healed as many as came to him; early the next day he moved on (Mark 1:21–39).[12] The activities of the day show Jesus communicating the rule of God by discourse in the morning and by the action of healing in the evening. Disciples were learning from him how to bear witness.

---

11. See, for example, John Dominic Crossan, *Jesus: A Revolutionary Biography* (San Francisco: HarperSanFrancisco, 1994). Even if this were overstated, it helps situate Jesus in his first-century Jewish Palestinian context influenced by Greek culture.

12. See Gerhard Lohfink, *Jesus of Nazareth: What He Wanted, Who He Was* (Collegeville, MN: Liturgical Press, 2012), 6–8.

The parables of Jesus offer an important lesson for those to whom they are addressed, especially when one can isolate the core of a parable that may reflect Jesus's own telling. Is a given parable aimed at individuals, or certain groups, or to Israel as a whole people of God? Sometimes one cannot be sure, or both are possibilities, and the difference may or may not be significant. But Jesus's concern for a corporate consciousness can never be far from the original intent. The social character of the message to Israel takes on an accented character in an individualist American culture; an explicit social meaning has to be underlined. One cannot separate a personal individual meaning of Jesus's teaching on the rule of God from its social implications. The stronger the sense of dignity of the individual, the stronger the need for social bonds and concern for tending them. The relationship raised by this story goes to the essential social character of human existence. Individual responsibility can never be completely separated from society, its relationships, and its values.

The parable of the Rich Man and Lazarus provides an example of different layers of meaning according to the addressee. On an individual level, it engages the status of rich persons and severely handicapped poor people. The rich man does not attend to the mandates of Torah, is deemed personally responsible before God by omission, and is appropriately condemned. The poor man, who has a name indicating his personhood, is otherwise deprived of an identity. He appears as everyone robbed of dignity by society. As one who suffers in this world and cannot help himself, he will have his reward in the end. This seems like standard religious reasoning. On the social level, however, the parable questions society itself, Israel. Has the rule of God any effect on a community in which this could take place? In addressing society, the parable pokes everyone's conscience by looking at suffering from a perspective of social responsibility.

Jesus's teaching also bears a symbolic meaning. Symbol refers to a particular thing, event, person, idea, or story that, while being intelligible in itself, offers a meaning about something other than itself. The relationship between these two persons, as individuals and within the context of a social relationship, bears a structural analogy to many other relationships of advantage and heedlessness, concern and neglect, power and abuse. They may refer to friend and enemy, neighbor and foreigner, boss and worker, white and Black. They reflect some pattern in a society and thus characterize it as social sin. This form of communication questions what people take for granted, tolerate, or promote. Jesus's teachings have a prophetic edge.

On the social symbolic level, the story of the rich man and Lazarus bears universal relevance to all communities. It also asks probing questions: How are we doing as a community? Can we imagine, if not calculate, the damage done by an unjust balance of possibilities and means in social relations? The questions break through the shield of individualism that isolates one by saying, "I'm not interested." They appeal to social awareness and afflict conscience. When the questions do not so penetrate the surface, they turn against and condemn the community that supports unjust relationships.

The consideration of a symbolic level of meaning shows that the story of the rich man (privileged, credentialed, powerful, influential, and person) and Lazarus (disabled, discredited, without leverage, marginalized, and treated as a non-person) cannot be limited to the simple binaries of rich and poor, good and bad, heaven and hell. It overlaps with all the stories about relationships between the strong and the disempowered. All the polarities are present in the inter-relationship between rich and poor on both personal and social levels. The binary of race in America, white and Black, is included in this story.

To sum up the way Jesus represented the rule of God with his teaching, one might ask what this story holds up to the imagination vis-à-vis racism. An inner circle of mutual influence links personal consciousness, society, and God; all religious consciousness is simultaneously conscious of self and world. The Christian tradition insists that human existence bears an image of God; but our particular human experience reinforced by society creates our image of God. We imagine God in our own image and likeness unless something crashes in and interrupts everything. Those who enjoy the power and social position to defend themselves tend to forget society's role in their good fortune and to think in terms of their individual agency. They ask whose fault lies behind each poor person, white or Black, and conclude that all people are now autonomously on their own. The pattern seems automatic and spontaneous.

By contrast, the story of rich and poor represents a large symbolic sense of God as caring for all and supporting a mutual sense of responsibility for one another. Contemplation of this story told by Jesus asks about one's place in the world, in existence, and as a member of society. It cannot view others apart from their social context (colorblindness), or the self as a private individual. It elicits a response that cannot be siloed; it cannot be dissolved into a relationship between me and God. It has to include my standing in a socially constituted world: responsible for my self and to the world. In the United States, this is a world of reciprocally related whites and Blacks. As was suggested in Chapter III, the realism of this meditation for racism in America can be achieved only by consideration of racist narratives. Summarizing Ellacuría's historical thinking on this, Ashley writes: "Now, to 'historicize' a concept or a set of concepts... means to understand it as [1] a part of an ongoing historical process, [2] to grasp how its usage interacts with, resists, or transforms the various dynamisms that constitute one's own specific historical situation, and finally, [3] to hold oneself accountable to the way that this understanding leads one to act (or fail to act) in that situation."[13] This story of Jesus forces the Christian to attend to racist narratives and to think in terms of actual history; the anti-racist power of Jesus's parables directs the imagination to actual history.

Jesus as Prophet

> A man fell victim to robbers as he went down from Jerusalem to Jericho. They stripped and beat him and went off leaving him half-dead. A priest happened to be going down that road, but when he saw him, he passed by on the opposite side. Likewise, a Levite.... But a Samaritan traveler who came upon him was moved with compassion at the sight. He approached the victim, poured oil and wine over his wounds and bandaged them. Then he lifted him up on his own animal, took him to an inn and cared for him. (Luke 10:30–34)

The gospels portray Jesus as a prophet. The role of prophet provides another reading of Jesus and how he functions in present-day Christian consciousness. It represents another

---

13. J. Matthew Ashley, "Contemplation in the Action of Justice: Ignacio Ellacuría and Ignatian Spirituality," in *Love That Produces Hope: The Thought of Ignacio Ellacuría*, ed. Kevin F. Burke and Robert Lassalle-Klein (Collegeville, MN: Liturgical Press, 2006), 146.

distinctive way of interpreting his teaching today. Seeing Jesus as prophet makes him particularly relevant in a situation of social sin.

The Hebrew scriptures provide the background for various attributes that would identify Jesus as prophet in his context. The prophet mediated, represented, declared, or delivered the word of God on a given topic. He was not a leader of worship, not an ethicist, not an explainer of the tradition or the law, but one who declared the perspective of God on the situation. If he was authentic, he was regarded as a spokesperson for God. The prophet had various ways of access to God's word through the initiative of God as Spirit, in visions or dreams, in the stories of the past, and by other intuitive or religious experiences. The category of prophet pointed mainly to a public persona, and prophecy had social relevance. In scripture, prophets were classical charismatic figures and prophecy was also an office and function. Prophets could cautiously counter the views of kings, priests, and other authorities or raise a public outcry. The role of prophecy developed over time, and prophets were not all the same, but the category is particularly relevant in times of social conflict.[14]

During his ministry, Jesus was regarded by many as a prophet. The gospels present him as the final prophet, although exegetes debate the degree to which he considered himself in that way during his ministry. To place him in that role provides a way of reading his teaching and actions. The

---

14. History offers many cases of lowercase prophets who perform a prophetic role of critique of society by bringing to bear God's perspective on situations. They usually disturb the status quo because God's word does not represent a human perspective of self-interest but a more "objective" view that strives to transcend a partisan stance.

prophetic function fits within the idea of revelation in which a historical agent becomes the medium through which the public receives an interpretation of God's perspective on things.

Ignacio Ellacuría spontaneously recognized the prophetic role of Jesus. Jesus's whole ministry is a proclamation of the rule of God in contrast to a negative historical situation in which some thrive at the expense of others. "For example, if the [rule of God] proclaims the fullness of life and the rejection of death, and if the historical situation of human beings and of structures is the [rule] of death and the negation of life, the contrast is evident."[15] Ellacuría uses the idea of utopia as a positive horizon of life in history constituted by social justice. Prophecy then becomes a method of thinking, a critical application of the judgment of the rule of God that can be translated into concrete goals and striven for.[16]

We turn now to Jesus's parable of the Good Samaritan, which some may not consider a distinctly prophetic teaching but which has prophetic power. First, though, a brief introduction to the narrative message of this classic story will be helpful. Luke sets the story up with a question from a lawyer. In the basic commandment of the love of God and of the neighbor as oneself, the lawyer wants Jesus's definition of the neighbor. The story then relates how two officers of

---

15. Ignacio Ellacuría, "Utopia and Prophecy in Latin America," in *Mysterium Liberationis: Fundamental Concepts of Liberation Theology*, ed. Ignacio Ellacuría and Jon Sobrino (Maryknoll, NY: Orbis Books, 1993), 292.

16. Ellacuría, "Utopia and Prophecy in Latin America," 290. The dialectical thinking here is analogous to the logic of the negative experience of contrast that was described earlier: the negative situation, in contrast to what should be, impels action to relieve the negation.

the temple bypass a man who has been assaulted along the road. It then completely exceeds what the law requires by describing how a Samaritan goes out of his way to help the presumed Jew and then assume responsibility for his recuperation.

Consider how the story must have fallen on Jewish ears. The story sets the standard for "neighbors" by a desire to find and create them rather than simply recognize those who are familiar. Jesus sets the high moral standard by using a non-Jew as the model. Jews should mold their ethical ideals on this enemy among enemies. The story criticizes Jewish religious leaders on the presumption that they had religious motives for avoiding the wounded victim. But, even on the surface, the story criticizes a piety that ignores practical help for one in distress. The story affirms that one should positively love one's enemies, and that failure to help anyone in serious need is a sin of omission, not because it is commanded, but because the imperative comes from within human existence itself. The fundamental level of urgency transcends a casuist's calculation of human responsibility.

The story of the Samaritan is standard Christian teaching of a high moral ideal. But Karl Rahner raises the stakes of the moral injunction of love of neighbor with a thesis on the closest conjunction and, at bottom, the identity of love of God and love of neighbor. He argues that "the categorized explicit love of neighbor is the primary act of the love of God."[17] The

---

17. Karl Rahner, "Reflections on the Unity of the Love of Neighbor and the Love of God," in *Theological Investigations* (Baltimore: Helicon Press, 1974), 6:247. Catherine of Siena delivered the same message. Failure to love neighbor is positive failure; lack of love of neighbor is negative because of an opportunity lost to love

reasoning of Rahner finds its grounding in the compound dynamic relations between God, world, and each human person. From a Christian perspective, the three are wedded together in a differentiated unity of influence and exchange.[18] They thus interact with each other in distinct ways but with mutual entailment. This metaphysics gives rise to Rahner's thesis that seems extreme but only on the surface. He summarizes it in this way: "It is radically true, i.e., by an ontological and not merely 'moral' or psychological necessity, that whoever does not love the brother whom he 'sees,' also cannot love God whom he does not see, and that one can love God whom one does not see only *by* loving one's visible brother lovingly."[19] Rahner thus gives the sayings of the Johannine writings metaphysical depth. He attributes utmost seriousness to a well-known and often taken-for-granted Christian teaching and gives it universal value.

If Jesus was a prophet, it was not only on certain occasions. The title refers to his person and a dimension of his whole ministry. The symbolic social relevance of the love of

---

God through the neighbor. Catherine of Siena, *Catherine of Siena: The Dialogue* (New York: Paulist Press, 1980), 34. She portrays God saying: "It is indeed true then, that every sin committed against me is done by means of your neighbors," 35.

18. This general statement can be parsed by individual relationships: to love the neighbor is part of the rule of God because each person belongs to God; to love God is to love God's own, which includes everyone; God's rule points to a community founded on loving respect for each other. The world is the medium of all these relationships.

19. Rahner, "Lover of Neighbor and Love of God," 247. Appreciation of this view requires a recognition that deliberate human actions reflect the fundamental self-disposition of a person; they shape and define each person. Rahner took the exercise of freedom very seriously.

neighbors that extends to love of enemies expands human responsibility in a positive and constructive way into public life and the sphere of the common good. It bears both social judgment and constructive human possibility. For example, at the very least, a response to a mugging along a commonly used road requires that the route be made safe for future travelers. This humane moral response runs before consideration of the mechanics of how this is to be done; the common social reaction exists prior to the debate about means to an end. Spontaneous spiritual concern goes out to potential future victims. Although the mechanisms of social efficacy differ historically, everyone should be concerned about common welfare.

In a modern democratic society in which racism permeates both social relationships and cultural thought and valuation, the moral and spiritual demands create a kind of dilemma. On the one hand, one cannot objectify the problem and assign it to other actors because it envelops the whole of society and culture. Society is everyone's concern. On the other hand, one cannot merely internalize a personal sentiment, but as a member one has to act out in some way one's revulsion at the social sin of one's own culture and society. When Jesus ended this story with the imperative to imitate the Samaritan, "Go and do likewise," he was announcing the inescapable spiritual demands of social belonging. One cannot have a moral society that protects the freedom of only some individuals without actual moral demands on all for social equality. Racism contains a latent accusation of omission on every member of society.

Some theologians puzzle over Jesus's commandment that people love one another: "A new commandment I give to you, that you love one another" (John 13:34). How can one command love, which rises up out of a person with spontaneity and sometimes surprise? But the fact that Jesus commands even love of enemies means that the character of love has to transcend the vagaries of feelings and sentiments that characterize it today. The commandment and the feeling of love can meet in a value response that recognizes the ontological value of the human person beneath his or her actions and that may be called respect for that personhood as such. While "respect" seems weak in comparison with many inflated notions of love, it prescribes a common reaction that transcends mere feelings and, as a positive response of valuing, would fulfill Jesus's command. It meets the radical prophetic ideal that Jesus sets forth in this story. On a personal level, it is impossible for all practically to love their enemies on an emotional level. But one can be challenged and reasonably respond to the rule of God that one respect the personhood of even one's enemy. On a social level, mindfulness of the value of the human person as a beloved creature of God will open the self to the moral and spiritual demands that racism places on all members of society.

Jesus as Healer

> As Jesus was entering a village, ten lepers met [him]. They stood at a distance from him and raised their voice, saying, "Jesus, Master! Have pity on us!" And when he saw them, he said, "Go show yourselves to the priests." As they were going they were cleansed. And one of them, realizing he had been healed, returned, glorifying God in a loud voice. (Luke 17:12–15)

Jesus was a healer. As Luke's Peter says in a sermon: "He went about doing good and healing all that were oppressed by the devil" (Acts 10:38). The gospels are filled with stories of Jesus giving personal attention to individuals who were afflicted. This has considerable bearing on the question of racism, not by reference to the sickness of those who were healed but for the attention of the follower of Jesus on his concern for others in a way that included their physical well-being.

There is no doubt that Jesus was a healer and that by healing drew people to himself. John Meier pays close attention to the details of each story in recounting the so-called miracles of Jesus because, by the criteria of historicity, they most assuredly made up part of his ministry.[20] But he goes on to say that in almost every case it is impossible to know exactly what happened in a miraculous event or how it was accomplished. There was a time when the miracle stories were taken as accurate historical accounts of the events as they appeared to observers. In the light of emerging physical sciences, miracle stories seemed to offer rationalistic proof of Jesus's divine power by breaking scientific laws of operation. But a critical historical study of scripture shows that the literary genre of a gospel does not aim at historical reportage but at communicating the content of faith. This straightforward recognition not only bypasses any critique from science, it also relieves the pressure one might feel about miracles in a scientific age. The stories do not communicate facts that caused faith but express the faith of the storytellers.

This twisting history leaves us with realistic creative tension rather than impasse. We know that Jesus cared for people on an individual basis and healed them. But we do

---

20. John P. Meier, *A Marginal Jew: Rethinking the Historical Jesus,* Vol. 2, *Mentor, Message, and Miracles* (New York: Doubleday, 1994).

not and cannot explain what exactly was going on in the incidents. The scripture has Jesus say relative to these wonderful deeds that "your faith has made you well" (Luke 17:19). But faith healing too is contentious, and how exactly Jesus healed in each case remains unknown. At the same time, Jesus mediated to people not only spiritual consolation; he also affected their whole persons. Jesus mediated material well-being as an intrinsic part of his ministry. One cannot compartmentalize God's relation to us and human response into a spiritual realm separate from ordinary life in the world.

The way God's presence, grace, and salvation come to bear on people requires some conversation. What can be extrapolated from the narratives of Jesus healing to the question of how that healing might be understood today? The liberation theology of Latin America has generated some incisive ideas on this issue. Gustavo Gutiérrez broke new ground when he explained how God's salvation affects human beings in the world as a positive influence and force in their historical existence. Christian experience bears witness to three levels or dimensions of this power. The creative power of God provides a foundation for the conscious freedom that marks human existence. The desire for emancipation and political freedom expands that freedom socially. And Jesus's mediation of God's forgiveness of sin and the power to resist systemic sin fulfills actual human existence.[21] This makes the struggle for social justice "part of a saving

---

21. Gustavo Gutiérrez, *A Theology of Liberation: History, Politics and Salvation* (Maryknoll, NY: Orbis Books, 1973), 153–60, 168–78. Walter Rauschenbusch, *A Theology for the Social Gospel* (New York/Nashville: Abingdon Press, 1945 [originally 1918]), very clearly expressed these views.

process which embraces the whole of man and all human history."[22]

Ignacio Ellacuría develops these ideas further. With his principle of historicization noted earlier, he makes the fundamental insight accessible to one doing the Exercises. Historicization means measuring the truth of ideas and the authenticity of intentions by their being turned into action. Expanding that principle to include salvation yields the conviction that became a maxim in his theology: Salvation in history is salvation of history. This means that salvation cannot be reduced to an internal spiritual effect of God's love and forgiveness; to be really appropriated it has to be turned into action. "It is not just that salvation history entails salvation in history as a corollary. Rather, the salvation of man in history is the one and only way in which salvation history can reach its culmination."[23] With this large statement about the workings of history, Ellacuría maintains that persons who experience the salvation mediated by Jesus should recognize that it entails responding to God's power that always works in the direction of social justice through agents.[24]

In a culture that prizes the private character of each person's faith it becomes difficult to maintain that an overt concern for social justice constitutes an essential characteristic

---

22. Gutiérrez, *A Theology of Liberation*, 160. "The growth of the [rule of God] is a process which occurs historically in liberation, insofar as liberation means a greater fulfillment of man." *A Theology of Liberation*, 177.

23. Ignacio Ellacuría, "Salvation History as a Salvation in History," in *Freedom Made Flesh: The Mission of Christ and His Church* (Maryknoll, NY: Orbis Books, 1976), 18.

24. Ignacio Ellacuría, "The Historicity of Christian Salvation," in *Mysterium Liberationis: Fundamental Concepts of Liberation Theology*, ed. I. Ellacuría and J. Sobrino (Maryknoll, NY: Orbis Books, 1993), 282.

of Christian faith. People may ignore it or block it out, but reflection cannot escape the inner imperative that Jesus's ministry elicits. Physical healing formed an intrinsic dimension of his ministry because it externalized his understanding of the rule of God. The stories of Jesus healing bear significance for social suffering and mending the common good. But to make this point, we should first look at the significance of the lepers.

The story of Jesus healing the lepers, when the imagination dwells upon it as Ignatius prescribes, yields both similarity and difference with the situation of racism. Lepers were afflicted with a physical disease that was considered contagious. Thus, lepers were isolated from daily commerce, stigmatized, marginalized by law, shunned, and excluded from society. At other times they were forced to live together in their own community. When Jesus cured the lepers of their physical disease, they were able to pass the test of scrutiny and could rejoin society.

Comparing and contrasting racism with the exclusion and marginalization accorded lepers is instructive. The marginalization is not based on something physically threatening like disease but, in Michelle Alexander's words, refers to "a stigmatized racial group locked into an inferior position by law and custom" because of skin color.[25] The system may not entail hatred or personal animus; it subsists in objective structures, is legitimated by laws and common patterns of behavior, and is more likely sustained by the indifference of many and the intent of few. Jesus cured lepers physically and it allowed for social integration. If racism is a disease, who are the afflicted? The question turns the story of the cure of

_____

25. Michelle Alexander, *The New Jim Crow: Mass Incarceration in the Age of Colorblindness* (New York: The New Press, 2020), 15.

the lepers into an antonym. Those with power and position who do not act have the disease. The cure lies in members of society becoming concerned enough to join the resistance to social bias and marginalization.

Ignatius designed the contemplations in the Exercises with a set of preparations. One of them consists of setting a scene and narrative in one's imagination in a way that puts a person in the scene as a participant observer. This creates an imaginative situation that allows what Ewert Cousins calls "the mysticism of the concrete event."[26] Establishing a scene in one's imagination creates a kind of realistic appreciation of the communicating event. Sometimes it entails focusing attention on certain figures in the contemplated scene. Another preparatory step consists in formulating a desired outcome of the contemplation. Fixing its goal establishes intentionality and helps prepare a person to both look for something and be ready to receive it.

Setting the social sin of racism as the context for the Exercises shifts the dynamics of what one might look for in the Exercises in a way that appears especially motivating in the healing stories. One can identify with the healer or the healed. The perspective of the disciple gravitates to the healer as the one to be followed; the active follower of Jesus thus identifies with the disciples as distinct from identifying with the beneficiaries of the healing. While this can hardly be a choice of one against the other, either/or, the distinction points to really different emphases. One leaves the First Week after serious engagement with sin and forgiveness. One who enters the Second Week does not ask

---

26. Ewert H. Cousins, "Franciscan Roots of Ignatian Meditation," in *Ignatian Spirituality in a Secular Age*, ed. George P. Schner (Waterloo, ON: Wilfrid Laurier University Press, 1984), 60.

for forgiveness for racism but for inspiration to find a direction in one's life through consideration of the ministry of Jesus of Nazareth. The Exercises are a spiritual school for realistic engagement and action. The disciple seeks to identify with Jesus and be concerned about the structure of a society that favors some at the expense of others.

Jesus as Standard for Christian Existence

The subheading of this chapter captures its theme: the logic of the Second Week of the Spiritual Exercises in the face of racism. We conclude the chapter by drawing together the elements and dynamics of the basic structure of Christian existence described thus far.

Jesus mediates a presence and an encounter with God less by words about God and more by the collected elements of his ministry to the rule of God found in the gospels. His revealing takes the form of a narrative, and his actions depict the rule of God. Ignatius demonstrates this by building his Exercises on the gospel stories about Jesus and the stories that Jesus told. Ignatius thus illustrates the truism that Christian faith essentially proposes a way of life rather than a set of beliefs or doctrines. In a large frame of reference, one can look upon Christianity as a movement within history.

Jesus began this movement by representing the rule of God and gathering disciples to help him mediate it. The program, if it can so be called, consisted in teaching and preaching, critically questioning anti-social behaviors, and attending to the discrete needs of people. Although interpretations of his identity whirled around him, he stayed the course of his ministry to the end.

Ignatius provides a way of encompassing in a single metaphor the inseparable other side of God's relation to existence: the standing of human beings and the world before or in the face of God. He calls this a "standard," a type of existence defined in contrast to the typical structure of a sinful life. The rule of God stands opposed to the rule of Satan (SE, 136–48).[27] In this interpretation of the Exercises, the standard of the rule of God is placed in contrast to racism. Racism is social sin with a long history, with roots that draw toxic nourishment from white supremacy and a power that infects a whole culture and society. Sometimes this breaks out into public view, but more deeply it works under cover of law and good order. Even the Constitution of the United States is infected with an invisible individualism that poses as enlightened, and in some ways is, along with its tolerance of slavery.

Against the background of racism, the Second Week of the Exercises presents Jesus as a representation of the rule of God and a fuller way of life. The Christian conception of it is built on Jesus's teaching, his prophetic critique of social life, his care for each person he meets, and his social concern for Israel. It represents a moral universe, a social anthropology built on respect for the value of each person and on the call of God to all persons to look out for the needs of their fellow human beings.

---

27. The title of the exercise is instructive: "A Meditation on Two Standards, the One of Christ, Our Supreme Commander and Lord, the Other of Lucifer, the Mortal Enemy of Our Human Nature." This meditation resembles the exercise on "The Kingdom of Jesus Christ." It has a special role in the discernment of spirits and making major life-decisions and thus will receive attention in the following chapter.

V

Appropriating the Rule of God

It is one thing to learn about Jesus and another to appropriate Jesus's message of the rule of God and internalize it as one's own. This chapter continues to discuss the rule of God in the gospel, but in a way that fixes attention on how those using the Spiritual Exercises absorb Jesus's message.[1] It accents how representations of the content of the rule of God invite a person existentially to commit to discipleship according to their talent and context. It fixes on gospel texts that bring out various aspects of spiritual commitment. These involve a constant discernment of spirits and come to a climax in what Ignatius called an election. The background for the whole chapter, racism, continues to be the sin to which this interpretation of the gospel responds.

---

1. In this respect, Chapter IV relates to this chapter the way knowledge relates to decision and action. It corresponds to reflection followed by action, as is fitting for this discussion. But in many respects theology follows the praxis of faith as reflection upon it. The order of presentation here does not preclude the mutual exchange between the existential orders of knowledge and action.

The way the Spiritual Exercises lead a person or group to appropriate the message of Jesus broadly follows the deep structure of how Ignatius's program works. The working model that has been adapted here offers an appreciation of structural sin (Chapter III), a turn to Jesus of Nazareth for a positive account of what a Christian response looks like (Chapter IV), and motivation for a commitment to discipleship (Chapter V). What follows considers the anthropological sources for a decision to follow Jesus. The recognition of structural sin releases a positive impulse to react against it, guided by the ministry of Jesus. This brief map sets up the gospel stories considered in this chapter as leading to what Ignatius called a life-decision or reorientation of one's discipleship.

A negative experience of contrast discussed earlier refers to a spontaneous recognition that a given situation offends a basic sense of right and wrong: an intuitive moral sensibility.[2] Although such a situation may be explained by social and ethical analysis, the initial response draws upon a more primitive moral sense. It includes an equally basic desire that the situation be resolved, the wrong righted, and the situation redressed. The primitive potential for such a moral experience may be considered part of the equipment of humanity, a dimension of a categorical imperative that wells up from within and has a transcendental and absolute character. It reflects an instinctive moral recognition that systemic injustice against a group within a given society or community amounts to a threat against humanity itself.

Ellacuría's description of levels of moral sensibility bears some analogy to a negative experience of contrast.

---

2. See pages 78–79 above.

Although it does not expressly highlight the negative dimension of moral insight as strongly, it expands the perception of social injustice by noticing three degrees of social moral perception.[3] Ellacuría calls the first degree of appreciating social reality a *realization* of its "weight," a term that symbolizes recognition of the moral density involved. Society exists in a complex knot of actions, interests, and motivations that give it a moral character. A first and primary dimension of appreciating racism as gravely wrong consists of becoming aware of being involved in something that encompasses society and presses in on the self. The second degree of social moral perception involves a deeper reaction, which consists in *shouldering* the weight of racism. A personal moral sensibility kicks in so that one feels that one is involved in and engaged by the negative social situation. The moral dimension hits home and grabs hold of the self. This stage of moral awareness expands one's individual responsibility to the point at which it becomes, in the case of racism, part of one's consciousness of the larger social situation in which one exists. American culture consists of whites and Blacks confronting each other in a power differential that is injurious to Blacks; it surrounds and embraces American thinking. Everyone participates in this situation. Ellacuría calls the third degree of moral response a *taking charge of* the weight of reality; it consists of a self-disposition relative to the situation

---

3. The analogy described here does not spring from a one-to-one comparison of the dimensions of experience drawn from critical theory and described by Edward Schillebeeckx and the dimensions Ellacuría learned from the philosophy of Xavier Zubiri. I know of no literary dependence. The analogy is grounded in the human reaction to social injustice, the consciousness of people who react against social suffering.

by a decision that becomes a form of action. This conscious reaction finds its place in Ignatius's Spiritual Exercises in the constant process of discernment of spirits and an election or appropriate life-decision.[4]

I noted in the preface the parallelism between the three stages of the Exercises and the elements of a negative experience of contrast as Edward Schillebeeckx describes it.[5] In the face of dehumanizing social structures, human consciousness instinctively recoils and seeks for ways to right the wrong. The natural mechanism reflects the foundation of a moral sensibility that, on the level of society and using Kantian language, elicits a categorical imperative. Both of these accounts of the groundwork of moral sensibility, by Edward Schillebeeckx and Ignacio Ellacuría, credit human beings with a moral intelligence that is capable of appraising objective social situations that are unjust and reacting against them. Both try to analyze something intrinsic to human existence, part of the native equipment of the species, that takes account of social injustice and reacts against it, prior to any social diagnosis or detailed knowledge of how to change the situation. One who directs or who does the Exercises in a situation of social injustice can appeal to this primitive a priori disposition. These structural anthropological analyses have a bearing on the logic of the Exercises when they clarify how a person moves from a recognition of structural sin to a reaction against it.

A second and deeper positive stimulus to a subjective appropriation of the rule of God lies in Jesus's ministry as

---

4. This description of Ellacuría's analysis of the dynamics of moral response to social reality is drawn from Kevin Burke, *The Ground beneath the Cross: The Theology of Ignacio Ellacuría* (Washington, DC: Georgetown University Press, 2000), 100–108.

5. See preface, page xvii.

preserved in the gospels. If Christian spirituality consists of following Jesus, then, at bottom, Jesus should be the inspiration for Christian life. But this role has some inbuilt conditions. To be the inspiration for human life, Jesus must be a genuine representative of human existence. Ignatius was quite deliberate in setting up the Second Week by likening Jesus to an archetypal human leader. The more Jesus is looked upon in terms that distinguish him from common human existence, the more he loses his ability to credibly model human life. On this point, Schillebeeckx and Ellacuría agree that God must be found in history, in the physicality of life and the relational exchange of human life together. The considerations that follow show Jesus attracting disciples and provide examples of how Jesus's parables inspire life motivated by the rule of God. Ignatius's use of the imagination to set realistic scenes of Jesus's ministry help to engender a realism in the historical contemplations.

Jesus Gathered Disciples

> As he was walking by the Sea of Galilee, he saw two brothers, Simon who is called Peter, and his brother Andrew, casting a net into the sea; they were fishermen. He said to them, "Come after me, and I will make you fishers of people." At once they left their nets and followed him.
>
> (Matt 4:18–20)

Jesus gathered disciples who followed him, learned from him, and went out on their own to do what he did. This seems to indicate that he was interested in stimulating a historical movement. This does not imply a desire to start what later became the church, but it suggests that Jesus wanted to have more than an impact on individuals in his religious society and culture. As it turned out, he became the inspiration for an energetic religious group within Judaism. Disciples were the link between Jesus's ministry and the church that finally emerged.

Disciples carry forward the spiritual and theological significance of Jesus whom they follow. Such a historical movement will involve various levels of participation, from active engagement in the project of Jesus to a loyal but more passive attachment. The discipleship found in the gospels consisted of active participation in Jesus's ministry. These were the men and women who accompanied him through the villages bringing the good news of the rule of God (Luke 8:1–3). On the one hand, some theologians cannot conceive of a passive following of Jesus or of passively being a Christian. Jesus and the rule of God intrinsically ask for active commitment.[6] On the other hand, we must imagine that, in the beginning as it is today, the engagement of the followers of Jesus ranged from intense and active to casual and passive, from missionary commitment to occasional assembly and less attention paid apart from it. The distinction does not aim at parsing and grading Christian affiliation.[7] It rather underlines the point that discipleship in the gospels carries the meaning of active intentional par-

---

6. Juan Luis Segundo, *The Community Called Church* (Maryknoll, NY: Orbis Books, 1973), 78–86, 89–91.

7. Discipleship requires some external actions, but it cannot be measured by these alone. Christian leadership, office holding, public appearance, or special kinds of activity require intention, and the authenticity of discipleship, while not a fully public category, requires some level of spiritual commitment, loyalty, dedication, and other inner virtues.

ticipation in Jesus's project. The disciples were those who actively joined Jesus in his ministry. The invitation extends to all, but to each according to his or her capacity.

The spiritual exercise entitled "The Contemplation of the Kingdom of Jesus Christ" (SE, 91–100) shows that Ignatius had an intentional level of discipleship in mind when he invited those making the Exercises into the sphere of the ministry of Jesus. The exercise sets the tone of the whole of the Second Week and, through it, of the whole program of the Exercises. The intention is explicit, and his own experience, as recounted in "The Autobiography," backs it.[8] Like a call to royal service in a special religious project the refusal of which would mean public disgrace, so too, but a fortiori relative to God's rule, the commitment should be absolute. The personal character of the call enhances the depth of the solicited commitment. On this premise, all the gospel stories presented for contemplation make an appeal for some kind of life-orienting commitment.

Disciples are often taught by internship; they learn by doing. This perspective opens up other dimensions of the Exercises. Jesus, as the central figure of the gospel stories, so dominates each scene that little explicit attention attaches to the disciple, with some exceptions. In many of the gospel stories they appear as the helpers of Jesus, his assistants, his collaborators who will then be sent out on mission. One can identify with them. One can imagine Jesus doing three things at once in some of the gospel stories: appealing to an audience, training fellow ministers, and inviting others to

---

8. "The Autobiography," *Ignatius of Loyola: The Spiritual Exercises and Selected Works*, ed. George E. Ganss (New York/Mahwah, NJ: Paulist Press, 1991), 65–111.

become active in the movement. The disciples are learning by being present to Jesus's ministry and participating in it. The gospels invite people to join a movement that spreads the Jesus-message to a wider audience.

Distinctions within discipleship permit a contrast between two different ways of entering into the contemplations of the Second Week. A person can imaginatively enter the scene of a gospel story as one seeking to become a beneficiary or a disciple of the teaching and ministry of Jesus. We will turn our attention to this distinction further on. While these perspectives are not exclusive and may work simultaneously, they are distinct enough to direct the conscious attention of the retreatant. Ignatius intends the Second Week for engaged disciples who are learning the ministry of Jesus in order to actively contribute to the project.

Ignacio Ellacuría helps to orient this active dimension of discipleship toward the social sin of racism. In his lecture notes on the Exercises, he says that the task of Christian spirituality as Ignatius has set it up is

> that of liberating the sin of the world and of constructing the new human person and the new world:
>
> > Once the sins of the world have been determined, the Christian attitude is one of struggle against it and against those who hold on to it oppressively; nonconformity and rebellion are consequently attitudes that are required for being Christians.
> >
> > The Christian task is also one of building up a new human person in constructing a new world, an attitude that sees in the cross of

Christ the way of resurrection and of the
presence of the reign of God.[9]

Although his words are directed against systemic structures that ensure the poverty of the many, they offer a ready
analogy within a racist society. Ellacuría goes on to say that
the Second Week of the Exercises constitutes the essence of
Christian life. "All the rest of the 'religious' elements are referred to this following, and take from it their value and
dimensions."[10]

The category of "disciple" in an Ignatian context thus
carries an extensive set of resonances that echo through the
program of four weeks. They amount to a summons to
Christian life, appealing to each individual within their particular situations. Its scope of service includes a social perspective. The call reaches out for a commitment that
involves active participation. The initial call offers only formal direction defined by a following of the historical Jesus;
this has to be interpreted in different historical contexts and
appropriated according to the abilities of a given individual.
But all disciples are united in a common attention to the stories of Jesus's ministry. They look for ways in which they can
be stimulated to actively participate in the movement more
than for what they might get out of attention to Jesus's ministry. This view of discipleship does not limit Jesus's appeal
to human freedom but opens it up to a wider horizon of possibility. There are as many ways of responding as there are
disciples. Christian discipleship includes distinct fellow actors, with distinct personal attributes, in distinct ways of life,

---

9. Ellacuría, "A Latin American Reading," 218.
10. Ellacuría, "A Latin American Reading," 220.

in distinct historical contexts: all called to actively follow Jesus of Nazareth.

Releasing Freedom for Creativity

> "Father, I have sinned against heaven and against you; I no longer deserve to be called your son." But his father ordered his servants, "Quickly bring the finest robe and put it on him; put a ring on his finger and sandals on his feet. Take the fattened calf and slaughter it. Then let us celebrate with a feast, because this son of mine was dead, and has come to life again; he was lost, and has been found." Then the celebration began. (Luke 15:21–24)

Many reasons help to explain why racism continues to have a hold on American society and culture. This chapter fixes attention on human subjectivity and motivation and examines where and how Christian faith might break in. The analysis of racism showed that it thrives on indifference, and indifference is supported by geographical segregation and unknowing.[11] Everyone is aware of the statistics of injustice, but distance supports inattention and encourages rationalization. One of those rationalizations builds on lack of power: Each one as an individual is impotent relative to a structural condition. It is what it is. Actual separations between whites and Blacks prevent whites from

---

11. Charles W. Mills, in *The Racial Contract* (Ithaca, NY: Cornell University Press, 1997), argues that within the political, moral, and epistemological contract of American society one finds a kind of intentional racial ignorance among whites that sustains self-deception or misunderstanding. See pp. 9–40 at 18–19.

converting a notional recognition of racism into a concrete reaction against it.

Turning to Christian faith, one has to ask how the stories of Jesus will be able to move people toward an active anti-racist attitude. Jesus's teaching and actions do not directly address the situations and problems of later times and places. Bringing Jesus forward into a racist context does not mean looking for words and actions that can be cited as referring to racist bias or practice. The gospels speak through the basic stories of Jesus. Finding that relevance may be better described as relating classic stories of Jesus that are well known and showing how they open the mind to take note of reality more deeply, stimulate interest, and motivate active concern about one's social milieu. Americans are surrounded by racial injustice. The dynamic of the stories of Jesus mediating the rule of God are familiar, but with an awareness of racism they can motivate and empower in a new way. Interpretations of four parables of Jesus within a historical context of racial injustice can help open up freedom to respond.

Reflection on the parables of Jesus provides a vehicle for getting close to the teaching of the historical Jesus. The parables also reflect the situations of the editors of the gospels. But the point of contemplations on the Jesus-stories far exceeds knowledge about him gained by tracing the lineage of the parables and exegesis. Contemplation introduces a personal dimension into the equation that affects the kind of knowledge that is mediated. It works with the texts and the persons contained in them through the imagination. Contemplation thus pushes beyond but not against critical history. The prayerful contemplations go beyond factual apprehension and "bring us not only to put ourselves in touch with Jesus but also to take upon ourselves what the reality of Jesus truly is and what it demands of us, and finally to take up an active stance (for or against) toward the reality of Jesus."[12]

The story called "The Prodigal Son," so called because of the reckless way the young man threw away his inheritance, could also be called "The Prodigal Father" because of the way his love for his younger son had no limits. The son was guilty of the gravest betrayal of the family, but it could not overcome the love of this father. That love restored life. Jesus states the point of the parable twice lest it be missed: The son was dead and now he is not only alive again but he will flourish within the father's love. The father's love exalts him. Two aspects of this story make it relevant to a person in the face of racism. The first lies in a person's coming to a new sense of self and one's agency, the second is a desire to serve others in gratitude. The first is highlighted by the text; the second is based on theological reflection. Experiencing God's love solidifies a new sense of self and a desire to serve others out of a newly found freedom. Martin Luther summed up the new freedom of the Christian who experiences God's love in two propositions: "A Christian is a perfectly free lord of all, subject to none. A Christian is a perfectly dutiful servant of all, subject to all."[13]

---

12. J. Matthew Ashley, "Ignacio Ellacuría and *The Spiritual Exercises* of Ignatius Loyola," *Theological Studies* 61 (2000): 36. Also, Ashley's *Renewing Theology: Ignatian Spirituality and Karl Rahner, Ignacio Ellacuría, and Pope Francis* (Notre Dame, IN: University of Notre Dame Press, 2022), 217.

13. Martin Luther, "The Freedom of a Christian," in *Luther's Works*, ed. H. J. Grimm (Philadelphia: Muhlenberg Press, 1963), 31:344. Ignatius's "Contemplation to Attain Love" (SE, 230–37) follows the same logic of gratitude.

The story of the Prodigal Son is almost a dramatization of Luther's pronouncement. At first, the young man, in finally realizing his predicament, thinks in rather pragmatic terms. His request of his father, that he be treated as one of his hired workers, carries minimal expectations compared with what he would receive. But the story shows the infinite excess of parental love, so that the son should have been able to expect more. The point of Jesus's telling is that God's love has no boundaries. The basic relationship of Creator to creature cannot be imagined apart from a dependence in being that is so imbued with love that it cannot be broken on God's part. God loves what God creates. The recognition mediated by the story so far exceeds the initial pragmatism of the son that it too is broken open. The imagined love of the father not only frees the son from his paralyzed state; the father's actual love gratuitously exalts the son within the family and society and gives him fuller agency.

The second dimension of the story makes it relevant to freedom in the face of structural sin over which an ordinary individual has little leverage. God's love and acceptance of persons authorizes, valorizes, and empowers their freedom when they are blocked by internal impediment or external circumstance. God's love stimulates the agency of freedom when it is disabled from within by self-preoccupation, frustration, or despair. The father dynamically symbolizes how the love of God for persons can draw freedom out of self-concern, even in the face of habitual routine. From the outside it seems like a paradox that freedom, totally dependent on God for its existence, can become autonomous in its own inner resources and resilient in resisting the structural status quo. Prophets and martyrs show precisely the way reception of God's attention to individuals can mobilize creative energy even against potentially mortal threats.

This first contemplation picks up the movement of the First Week of the Exercises, where the love of God appears as mercy and forgiveness. This story adds the themes of acceptance, authorization, and thereby a relationship that empowers the agency of freedom. Its relevance appeals to all, both Black and white. For the person who imagines that racism so dominates our social situation that personal freedom is swallowed up by it, the love of God for every human being stimulates the imagination to look for ways of becoming engaged.[14]

The Meaning of Justice

> Going out about five o'clock, [the landowner] found others standing around, and said to them, "Why do you stand here idle all day?" They answered, "Because no one has hired us." He said to them, "You too go into my vineyard." When it was evening the owner of the vineyard said to his foreman, "Summon the laborers and give them their pay, beginning with the last and ending with the first." When those who had started about five o'clock came, each received the usual daily wage. So when the first came,

---

14. There is more in this parable that has bearing on racism. The *ressentiment* of the brother blinded him to what he already possessed, a relationship of partnership and thus co-agency with his father in the whole enterprise of the family. He had the resources to participate in his father's exhilaration.

they thought that they would receive more, but each
of them also got the usual wage. (Matt 20:6–10)

The parable of the Laborers in the Vineyard does not on a
first reading communicate an accurate interpretation of its
full meaning. There are too many variables. The story contains a number of constituent parts: the householder, who
also owns land and a vineyard; a vineyard that always in
this context suggests Israel itself; early workers who agree
to a day's salary; and late workers who receive the same
salary. Choose any one of these elements as a principal
focus and the meaning of the story changes.

The story cannot be about business, about hiring, firing,
and fair pay, because it is about the kingdom of heaven,
which means the rule of God. If it includes business, the rule
of God cannot mean equal pay for unequal work, for this is
no way to run a business. It also fails as larger fiscal policy.
At the same time, it is obviously the case that the story is exactly about these things. We have to find the meaning in the
story and not behind it.

The several protagonists in the story make it liable to
being interpreted as an allegory in which each set of actors
stands for other groups in a backstory that is the real story;
the householder is God, and the early hires and the late hires
stand for other groups. Each person or group is assigned a
role that is justified in the rule of God. In this approach, binaries become an irresistible temptation, and they take over
the story: Jews and Christians, rich and poor, men and
women, whites and Blacks.

A way through these surface interpretations fixes first
on the parable as in some form going back to Jesus and de-
cides its meaning within the context of his ministry. Amy-Jill
Levine reads the story in the light of Jewish background ma-

terial and precedents from Jewish tradition.[15] Her analysis makes the parable coherent as a parable and not an allegory, applicable to the theme of this book, and prophetically challenging for Christians today.

Levine's analysis of the parable interprets it as another description of the rule of God. In the course of the story, it appears that the householder who owns the vineyard does contain a reference to God and God's rule, and these are indeed found in the way the householder behaves in his hiring practice. But a major difference between Jesus's meaning and the way it may be received in America today lies chiefly in the two socio-cultural contexts. To state it in an overly blunt and simple way: Jesus appealed to the corporate religious and cultural identity of Israel, whereas present-day America is individualist and competitive. The parable challenges a *quid pro quo* transactional view of justice and appeals to communitarian values. This short-hand diagnosis makes sense in Levine's actual analysis.

Levine interprets the parable as a description of God's ways, with the invitation that those who hear the parable imitate God's ways in the conduct of their affairs. The householder, who also runs a business, does symbolize God and the behavior of those who live by God's rule on earth. God loves all equally, and the offensive element of the story lies chiefly in the way the equality of love is portrayed. The owner of the vineyard is just by the letter of the agreement, as explained to those hired early. But in contractual terms he is generous to those in need, giving a family's living wage to those hired later who would otherwise suffer the loss of it. This is the loving rule of God extended to all. The twist in

---

15. Amy-Jill Levine, *Short Stories by Jesus: The Enigmatic Parables of a Controversial Rabbi* (New York: HarperCollins, 2014), 213–37.

this story is not God's injustice but God's love for all in their actual need, demonstrated in concrete action that surprises human expectation.

Doubts about this relatively straightforward interpretation lie at two junctures. The first has to do with a sense of community in contrast to thinking in terms of individual compensation. Levine gives examples of a corporate identity in Israel that recognized mutual solidarity. All receive the same reward because all take part in the work. All the soldiers enjoy the spoils of victory, even those who guarded the tents; all the players on the team—not just the stars—get the championship ring. Those who work together for the rule of God are not concerned about those who get more but about those who do not get enough.[16]

The other blockage may be found in the high moral standard of the rule of God. The parable challenges people in positions of authority who pay their employees. The parable considers employees as persons with their own responsibilities; the parable personalizes the salary rather than reducing it to a unit in an objective transaction with any individual. "The equality of his payment and thus his treating all the workers 'equally' derives from a sense of justice keyed into what people need to live."[17] The story, then, is less about egalitarianism or concern for fair pay, and more about the responsibility of those with power and the social systems in which we live. As in the story of the Good Samaritan, the rule of God here extends beyond the isolated example to an active seeking of more workers to share in the resources. The rule of God opposes mean-spiritedness and reaches out to invite more people into the abundance of shared life. In a racist sit-

---

16. Levine, *Short Stories by Jesus*, 234–35.

17. Levine, *Short Stories by Jesus*, 235.

uation, one cannot even begin to appreciate the impulse for social reparations when individualism and competing interests control the context for thinking.

But, like any altruistic and positive view of life, the rule of God leaves a residue of criticism, and in this story one finds it in those hired early. "The first hired do not want to be treated equally to the last; they want to be treated better."[18] This parable suggests something analogous in the context of American racism and the remnants of white supremacy. It awakens associations with the thread of *ressentiment* found in the analysis of racism and in the parallel reaction of the older brother in the parable of the Prodigal Son. It reflects competition rather than solidarity. A large part of American society suddenly cannot accept affirmative action because it offends the rights of individuals guarded by the American Constitution. A large space separates the vision of life proposed by the Constitution and the rule of God preached by Jesus of Nazareth. Surely they represent different spheres of life and have different functions, but more importantly, they illustrate different ideals of culture and community. Perhaps they should not be read in opposition to each other. But culturally, socially, and morally, the rule of God calls everyone to a higher spiritual level.

Commitment to the Common Good

> After a long time the master of those servants came back and settled accounts with them. The one who had received five talents came forward bringing the additional five. He said, "Master, you gave me five talents. See, I have made five more." His master said

---

18. Levine, *Short Stories by Jesus*, 231.

to him, "Well done, my good and faithful servant. Since you were faithful in small matters, I will give you great responsibilities. Come, share your master's joy." (Matt 25:19–21)

Like the previous parable, the parable of the Talents enters the world of financial transaction but makes a deeply humanistic point in relation to the rule of God. Commentators bring out various aspects of the biblical language, but many agree that the story urges active commitment to the rule of God. Contemplation or meditation on the story carries one more deeply into a relationship with God than the simple narrative of the transaction represents.

The structure of this story revolves around money, a large sum of money, entrusted by a man of wealth to servants or stewards in order to be worked in his absence. They have been delegated to manage, invest, or loan the money at interest for the benefit of the one for whom they work. The delegating sets up an existential relationship that can be viewed from the perspective of the wealthy man or those he commissioned. The relationship could be characterized as "command and obey," but it is more complicated. On the giver's part, it involves trust and expectation; on those entrusted with the money it involves a duty, a task, and an obligation to perform. The money is not a gift but an investment, and the servants have received an assignment. The one who empowers the stewards gives no instructions on how to deploy the money but, as the story indicates, it involves imagination and risk.

Practical interpreters of the parable often propose that the money given to the servants bears an analogy on an existential level with the abilities and personal gifts given to everyone, not simply as gifts but as resources. As the wealthy man entrusts his servants with his financial resources to work them into gain, so too the Creator bestows upon human beings personal assets to deploy in the advancement of the rule of God. Israelites, especially as enlisted into a covenant with God, and by extension all human beings as creatures, share as God's people the obligations of a bond holding them together, whether in terms of Torah or the rule of God that Jesus proposes. The sphere of Jesus's preaching almost automatically shifts the transactional language of financial obligation into commitment and loyalty to the rule of God. The analogy lies in trust and expectation across a completely transposed context. God entrusts something much more complicated than money in the creation of reflectively conscious human beings. It seems impossible not to make the comparison in the spiritual sphere of Jesus's teaching; the analogy cannot depend on the tenuous thread of the English word "talent."

What do the stewards of the money owe the one for whom they work? More, certainly, than a simple return of the money as illustrated in the case of the third person. The charge implies investment, action, and uncertainty: managing the money to increase it. The man commands something precarious, dependent on imagination, deliberation, decision, and action, along with hope that it will succeed and worry that it might not. The ones given the commission find themselves, with their particular abilities, thrown into a position that requires results. The situation itself demands some form of activity, and the persons involved cannot find recourse in passivity and evasion of responsibility.

The story's conclusion illustrates that the fundamental issue is not the amount of money that is earned. Both the first and the second steward were equally successful in doubling the owner's resources even though the sums involved were different. In contrast to both, the third person failed because he could not act in a manner that accepted the peril involved. Success and failure thus depend less on the resources than on the constructive use of whatever is given for the task. Failure has more to do with inaction than action, with passivity and omission rather than a bland misreading of the situation. In effect, ironically, the third person was condemned for doing nothing at all, but he was far from innocent. The point is that the rule of God consists of action; those who would be part of it assume responsibility through creative use of the resources they are provided. This story illustrates that failure consists of not doing something, of playing it safe, of not using the equipment one has been given, of failing to define the self and one's status of being as the agent one is created to be. The logic here is simple, but the charge reaches down to the rationale for one's existence.

The parable of the Talents directs attention to the rule of God. As a narrative metaphor of the rule of God it takes on explicit American relevance within life in a cultural and social situation of racism. The parable adds to the pool of meaning that other parables, aphorisms, teachings, and actions of Jesus have contributed to a self-understanding of free agents in the created world. Freedom, not only as deliberate choice but more importantly as self-orientation, commitment, and creative action, lies at the heart of the defining characteristics of human existence. The reflective ability to determine the specifics of people's individuality by their commitments and actions sets human persons apart from evolutionary ancestors. The ability of human groups to organize and set a course of action gives them an active role in social formation and evolution. This unique relationship of autonomy and dependence and on God as the ground of existence requires more than the gratitude shown by the single leper who returned to thank Jesus. The rule of God, which emerges from the Creator's intention, reflects an inner obligation, an imperative that rises up from existence itself and exceeds an obligation of mutual agreement, business contract, or direct command of authority. It places the care of social sectors in the hands of people and their leaders to steer structures toward the common good. The rule of God reflects a corporate imperative for social justice that freedom itself must construct; the rule of God includes each human being in a relationship of dependence upon the Creator and each other. It appeals to the active engagement of the unique resources that constitute the individual character of each person. In the voice of Jesus in this parable, the rule of God informs ignorance of the need for action; it acknowledges risk but does not accept fear as an excuse; and it condemns passivity on the basis of a corporate moral responsibility. The situation of racism positively lights up the relevance of these abstract descriptions of human responsibility.

But we must hope that the rule of God is gentler than in the case of the third steward of the parable of the Talents. The reaction of the businessman to the failure of his employee seems like deliberate exaggeration. But it urges the hearer to recognize the seriousness of the imperative, to register the resources that have been given each person, and to put them to work for structural justice, the common good. Although the phrase "common good" does not reach the grandeur of "the rule of God," it is the ordinary stuff from which the rule of God on earth is made.

An Eschatological Perspective (Matt 25:31–46)

> Then the righteous will answer him and say, "Lord, when did we see you hungry and feed you, or thirsty

and give you drink? When did we see you a stranger and welcome you, or naked and clothe you? When did we see you ill or in prison, and visit you?" And the king will say to them in reply, "Amen, I say to you, whatever you did for one of these least brothers of mine, you did for me."

(Matt 25:37–40)

The short text does not capture the scope of this passage from the gospel of Matthew entitled the "Parable of the Sheep and the Goats." It tells a story that portrays the judgment of all the nations, all people being saved or condemned at the culmination of time. Some do not regard it as a parable but as an apocalyptic revelation. John Donahue, after a review of the literary commentary, reads it as an apocalyptic parable because it has some qualities of a parable, but one that has to be interpreted within an apocalyptic framework.[19] Consideration of such a parable is appropriate here because apocalyptic literature "arises generally among people who are themselves suffering or oppressed" and thus require a sense of justice in the end.[20] This applies to individuals as well, and Ignatius explicitly appeals to an apocalyptic strategy in his discussion of how to make a life-decision. More on this latter point further on.

The whole parable turns on the criterion of salvation found in the words of Jesus who in the end-time is simulta-

---

19. John R. Donahue, "The 'Parable' of the Sheep and the Goats: A Challenge to Christian Ethics," *Theological Studies* 47 (1986): 10. Apocalyptic refers to a kind of literature that deals with the end of time, that includes judgment of good and evil and establishes the equilibrium of justice. In Jesus's ministry it also carries a sense of being imminent and even present and ready to break in.

20. Donahue, "The 'Parable' of the Sheep and the Goats," 29.

neously Son of Man,[21] king, and final judge. The criterion consists of whether or not one treated "the least of these my brethren" (Matt 25:40) with loving kindness when they were in extreme need and suffering (hungry, thirsty, aliens or alienated, naked, sick, or in prison). The list is repeated four times. The twist in the parable lies in the king's judgment: in reacting to these brothers, "you did it to me" (Matt 25:40). The criterion of salvation lies in reaction to Jesus and the rule of God he preached, but they are found hidden in "the least of his brothers."

The classic interpretation has been that Jesus's brothers were his disciples or, in the time of Matthew's community, Christian disciples who were bearing witness to Jesus's message of the rule of God. The context is a missionary church: "Go therefore and make disciples of all nations" (Matt 28:19). But since the nineteenth century more and more interpreters look upon anyone who is systematically despised as the brother of Jesus. Even more widely, treating other people with the respect they deserve as persons becomes the norm for salvation. These last two points penetrate deeply into something fundamental in the Christian imagination. It has its most direct statement in the principle of the mutual entailment of love of God and love of neighbor. One "who does not love his brother whom he has seen, cannot love God whom he has not seen" (1 John 4:20). When James Cone assimilates the lynched Black to Jesus crucified or Ignacio Ellacuría speaks of taking God's people down from the cross, this is

---

21. In the Book of Daniel, the Son of Man was seen in a vision as one to whom "was given dominion and glory and kingdom, [so] that all peoples, nations, and languages would serve him; his dominion is an everlasting dominion, which shall not pass away, and his kingdom one that shall not be destroyed" (Dan 7:14).

more than association of ideas. They are invoking an elementary principle. The parable makes this the criterion of salvation.

In Donahue's judgment, the weight of the textual evidence from the gospel's language, christology, and the concept of discipleship lean toward "the brothers of Jesus" referring to Christians who bear witness to being followers of Jesus. But at the same time, this confessional reading readily opens up to all human beings in a context of final judgment. The community of Christian faith supplies the context and perspective; but as an apocalyptic vision it encompasses all of history and appeals to the will of the Creator for all peoples. An apocalyptic vision of the future has two functions: it not only describes future judgment; it also reveals the norms that are operative in the judgment and should be at work in the world prior to the judgment. The parable of the Sheep and the Goats, therefore, lays down the community's expectations of the essential quality of Christian life: "The true order of justice is maintained when those acts of mercy and loving-kindness characterize the life of discipleship."[22] The parable thus contains "an ethic of faithful witness where the Christian, like Jesus in the proclamation of the gospel of the [rule of God], becomes the locus for the disclosure of God's will for all peoples."[23]

When this apocalyptic perspective is invoked in the context of meditation on the teaching of Jesus on the rule of God

---

22. Donahue, "The 'Parable' of the Sheep and the Goats," 24–25. This defines the ethics of the Christian community. "To be a Christian is to be actively engaged in confronting and alleviating the sufferings of those most afflicted in our society, since Christ identifies with them" (28).

23. Donahue, "The 'Parable' of the Sheep and the Goats," 30.

against the background of the structural sin of racism, it takes on piercing existential value. It clarifies complex situations with an implicit scale of values that measures things against a background of ultimacy. Ignatius was aware of this when he suggested that people may use their imaginations to project the time of their own death and the final judgment of God as a vehicle for making a life-decision.

> I will consider, as if I were at the point of death, what procedure and norm I will at that time wish I had used in the manner of making the present election. Then, guiding myself by that norm, I should make my decision on the whole matter. (SE, 186)

> Imagining and considering how I will find myself on judgment day, I will think how at that time I will wish I had decided in regard to the present matter. And the rule which I will then wish I had followed is what I shall apply now, in order that then I may be in complete contentment and joy. (SE, 187)

This imaginative meditative practice plunges one into a world of values that help a person to sift through the myriad circumstances of life. The context of ultimacy allows one to take actual historical conditions seriously. It also pushes the imagination to go well beyond them to consider, project, deliberate, and evaluate courses of action and consequences. It forces reflection on one's life as a narrative up to the present time and then to a penultimate future. The process empowers a person before God to decipher more deeply who one is and who one wants to be. Such is the question that one has to ask in the face of the racist character of American life.

Historical Discernment of Spirits

We have been tracing the Spiritual Exercises according to a three-part logic of exposing sin, turning to Jesus as a revelation of the rule of God as antithetical to sin, and internalizing Jesus and his message. From the beginning of his conversion, Ignatius had to wrestle with the flood of thoughts and feelings that the impulse to change his life's direction had let loose within himself. Managing the internal conflict led Ignatius to consider principles and maxims that enable one to sort through feelings, thoughts, and the motives that accompany spiritual motivation.

We saw that, in dealing with sin, the shift of perspective from personal to structural sin engages a different kind of responsibility. So too in the question of the discernment of spirits, the focus on the sin lodged in social structures occasions a distinctive appeal to the imagination, one that differs from Ignatius's framework of individual self-analysis. Steering the Spiritual Exercises along the path of structural sin requires adjustments in the program contained in Ignatius's text, which concentrates attention on personal sin, responsibility, a sense of guilt, and forgiveness. Structural sin carries social pressure; it implicates a person in something seemingly outside the self in indirect, historical, and institutional ways. It requires more objective forms of accountability and resistance. Just as in the First Week, so too in the matter of responding to sin through positive discernment and decision, the analysis needs both Ignatius's insight into subjective discernment of spirits and a more objective social analysis of the dynamics of social sin and how one relates to social action against it. The distinct focus on racism occasions a social form of discerning "the spirits" and a more public range of considerations for decision-making. In short, a focus on social responsibility shifts the way one appreciates and internalizes the implications of Jesus's ministry for one's own life.

Ignatius's Spiritual Exercises provide two distinct ways in which the person making them can dwell on the question of how to apply the rule of God manifested in Jesus's ministry to one's own life. The first way is contained in "The Rules for the Discernment of Spirits" (SE, 313–27, 328–36), which supply formal but direct questions about one's motivation. The process consists of maxims for recognizing how the spirits operate within the self. They enable reflective consideration and deliberately engage one in the process of internalizing Jesus's message. The first way focuses on direct reflection on one's personal life. The rules reflect Ignatius's own experience of sorting out the factors that were operative in his lengthy conversion experience. They are meant as guidelines to correlate one's experiential life with the rule of God against the many obstructions to freedom.[24] The second way is more spontaneous because, rather than being expressed in formal maxims, it is factored into the whole series of the contemplations of Jesus's ministry. The second process is set up in the meditation on "The Two Standards," which contrasts what the ministry of Jesus stands for with what the mythic symbol of Satan stands for (SE, 136–47). This method of discernment operates in the contrast of the ministry of Jesus with the imagined strategy of Satan. The standard of Christ presents a narrative symbol of the rule of God as it appears in the more objective and

---

24. Ignatius placed his "Rules" outside the four-week structure of the Exercises in a section titled by editors as "Supplementary Materials." But they are meant to be operative across the whole course of the Exercises and beyond them as well. They become especially relevant, however, when a person is making a life-decision.

historical terms of the stories about Jesus against the forces of evil. The contrast provides a framework for aligning personal life in relation to structural sin.

Formal discernment of spirits. The rules for the discernment of spirits are two sets of maxims or counsels that help those making the Exercises and those assisting them to sort through the many feelings, images, ideas, and transcendent impulses that are occasioned by the meditations and contemplations. They are always operative. The primary structure of these rules is the binary between good and evil; it has correlates in a felt subjective orientation toward God, called consolation, and toward evil and chaos, called desolation.[25] These are clues for a proper response to God. The rules are elaborated to help persons sort out their basic instincts, impulses, and motivations in life generally, along the way of doing the Exercises and when making life-decisions or commitments for the future.

The criterion of the standard of Jesus. The second process of discernment revolves around the standard of Jesus represented especially during the contemplations of Jesus's ministry that take place during the Second Week. Jesus is proposed as a standard, a sign, or a symbol that functions as a type or characterization of how to respond to God, a representative of a life according to the rule of God. He stands in contrast to Lucifer and the way of "the world" that is hostile

---

25. Consolation and desolation also include the source from which and the direction toward which a feeling impels a person: toward God, like love of God, or, by contrast, a desire for base things antithetical to God's purposes (SE, 316–17). See Michael J. Buckley, "The Structure of the Rules for Discernment of Spirits," *The Way: Supplement* 20 (Autumn 1973), 28–29.

and opposed to the rule of God. The meditation on Two Standards proposes that Jesus and his ministry constitute a public, objective representation, a narrative mediation, of the character of the rule of God and what it looks like in human life.

How this criterion applies to the personal life of an individual doing the Exercises can be seen in the meditations "The Three Classes of Persons" (SE, 149–57) and "Three Ways of Being Humble" (SE, 165–68). Both meditations show how Jesus and his ministry act as criteria for guiding one's life or planning a life-decision. The meditation on the "Three Classes" proposes that a person act in a way that is solely motivated by service to God after the pattern of Jesus (SE, 155). In the consideration of degrees of humility, the highest form of life aligns motivation with a close imitation of Jesus (SE, 167). These two meditations show formally how this process of a discernment of spirits operates throughout the course of the Exercises and life itself. The preparation of each contemplation focuses on the subject matter, the ministry of Jesus, and the preparation of each contemplation asks that a person retrieve from the narrative an applicable insight into the rule of God for one's own life.

Historical discernment of spirits. Ignacio Ellacuría, in his extensive notes on a Latin American reading of the Spiritual Exercises, noticed that following Jesus and the rule of God required a specific historical consciousness that responded to the concrete world in which one was living. The world of repression and conflict itself required a discernment of spirits and a distinct historical reaction. At this point he did not turn to an extended analysis of Ignatius's rules for the discernment of spirits but said: "What is necessary is a historical discernment of spirits," and that the "orienting principles of this discernment are already there."[26] He was referring to the gospel stories of Jesus and their crystallization in the standard of Jesus in opposition to Satan. In other words, all the contemplations on the ministry of Jesus amount to a steady construction of the criterion of the rule of God. Jesus reveals the rule of God.

Ellacuría also looked at the motivational factors underlying the dynamics of the rule of Satan and found them operative in institutions, within the repressive cultural and social patterns of actual history. Wealth becomes the goal of life. Honor represents high social status above others. And pride issues in domination of others. "Resisting the hegemony of these principles and working to objectify and institutionalize an alternative vision is not 'just' a social-political project, but is at the core of the living out of Christian faith; it is a thoroughly 'spiritual' work."[27] The rule of Satan appears as organized opposition to the sociocultural incarnations of the rule of God; the standard of Jesus promotes service in the movement of the rule of God

---

26. Ellacuría, "Latin American Reading," *Spiritus* 10 (2010), 222. J. Matthew Ashley comments on what is going on here: "In short, using this meditation ['The Two Standards'] to frame the discussion of discernment provides the more natural avenue for producing an interpretation of the *Spiritual Exercises* that emphasizes its power as an instrument for 'historicizing' Christian faith on a social, corporate level." *Renewing Theology*, 205.

27. Ashley, *Renewing Theology*, 206. Note that personal and historical discernment of spirits are not mutually exclusive. Ellacuría says it plainly: "The disjunction between the personal and historical dimensions is a false one…. Finding God in the actualization of history is an essential problem for the theology, the pastoral action, and the spirituality that is demanded in Latin America today." Ellacuría, "Latin American Reading," 207.

and the construction of benevolent structures of an inclusive common good.

Ellacuría does not develop a set of rules for discerning how a person or group might form a life-plan to participate in the movement of the rule of God within history. But in his sixth lecture he describes what following the historical Jesus entails in a world of socially repressed human freedom. He retrieves the themes of Latin American liberation theology which have their analogues in Black liberation theology and are an antithesis to racism. For example:

> A world that permits and even requires that the greater part of the world is left out is, in itself, its own condemnation.

> If the historical condition for riches, honor and domination of a few is the poverty, disregard and humiliation of the many, then we have a maximum of irrationality and of destruction.

> The mutual alienation to which the two groups in struggle are subjected objectifies the profound failure of a world that is built on this dynamism.[28]

In sum, a Christian reaction against racism cannot be blind; it requires discernment. It must be as intentional as the rule of Satan when it operates within the structures of social and cultural history. It requires personal and, just as importantly, incisive historical discernment that feeds into a life-decision.

---

28. Ellacuría, "Latin American Reading," 226.

Life-Decision

The discernment of spirits orients a person toward and enables what Ignatius calls an "election." An election may or may not be a decision that is unchangeable, such as, in Ignatius's day, whether to embrace a married or clerical state in life. The suggested equivalent term, "life-decision," expresses the seriousness reflected in the process leading up to such a commitment and its effect on the person who makes such a decision. Ignatius takes time to propose how such decisions can be made (SE, 169–89). A fundamental maxim, always operative, says that what is decided be a means toward the larger goal of a person's ultimate destiny (SE, 169; also SE, 23). Such a decision is not an end in itself, but an enveloping orientation of life that provides an organizing principle, like an inner compass, that is at work even when one does not reflectively attend to it.

Ignatius briefly describes three notionally distinct ways for making such a decision.[29] The first kind of decision can be described as self-evident; the fittingness is so obvious that the decision seems to make itself or is made for one. Ignatius sees God's grace at work here. The second appeals to the deep experience or feeling of consolation that surrounds an option: a discernment of spirits in Ignatius's first formal sense aligns this decision with the rule of God. The "feeling" involved here does not lie on the surface like the

---

29. He calls them suitable "times." But they could also be considered different "kinds" because of the leading impetus for the decision. Having said this, it is equally important to not see them as exclusive or isolated from each other; they can work together, like distinct points of view, for a more elaborate process aiming at accurate representation. SE, 175–77.

feelings that come and go; it is the deeper conviction that words seek to express and may not be adequate. The third kind of decision is made in a time of tranquility that considers options, their comparative merits, and their consequences by critical analysis.[30] As noted in the discussion of discernment, these ways of deciding can best be used to help verify a given option. Michael Buckley draws "the times of election into some parallels with the various levels in the discernment of spirits."[31]

With an election the process of the Spiritual Exercises reaches a kind of apogee. More remains to be said and done, but a life-decision marks the new beginning aimed at by Ignatius: directing one's life by making a life-decision through discerned and ordered affections (SE, 21). The text of the Spiritual Exercises places this decision in the context of personal sin and the formation or reformation of one's personal life. By adjusting the Exercises to respond to a structural sin in the particular location of American history, the reorientation of one's life represents a new, specific, positive, and expansive commitment to the movement of the rule of God against American racism. The particulars of such a decision share in the individuality and situation of the one making the commitment, but they also participate in a much larger movement. As noted

---

30. Ignatius illustrates the third "time" of deliberation with two extended "methods" of proceeding. SE, 178–88.

31. Buckley, "The Rules for Discernment of Spirits," 35–36. Buckley sees transcendent illumination, intellectual reflection, and the attractions of affectivity as elements of a transcendental structure of religious experience. Ignatius provides an outline for a consistent religious anthropology (25). This means that the dynamics of discernment and decision-making are much more commonsensical than the scholarship that surrounds them suggests.

in the previous chapter, prophetic intention, decision, and action make the rule of God efficacious in history.[32] Although racism does not exhaust the full range of social sin in the world or in America, it has pervasive injurious effects on the whole of American life. Behavior that helps thwart that sin represents a worthy commitment of one's freedom in the various ways and degrees that the concrete situation allows.

Resurrection Hope

From the perspective of a person doing the Spiritual Exercises, a life-decision marks a decisive point in the process. But the open future always lies ahead and in absolute terms it raises a permanent question: Where am I going? And below its surface still another issue persists: Does one's decision make an ultimate difference? Asked by each one in our own ways, the question never really goes away. Is life worth living? The Christian walks into the future within the framework of what is celebrated each Easter season: the death and resurrection of Jesus.

A theological truism says that the death and resurrection of Jesus are tied together; never one without the other. On the side of death, Jesus's form of death places him with the wretched of the earth, tortured and executed. He represented God as on the side of those who suffer and died among them. But Jesus's resurrection vindicates the God of life.

Jesus believed in the resurrection. But his belief, ironically, does not provide the basis of Christian faith. That is

---

32. Ignacio Ellacuría, "Utopia and Prophecy in Latin America," *Mysterium Liberationis: Fundamental Concepts of Liberation Theology*, ed. Ignacio Ellacuría and Jon Sobrino (Maryknoll, NY: Orbis Books, 1993), 293.

found in the conviction about his destiny. In a brief period after Jesus's death, itself unable to be measured, those who were in shock at his execution gradually came to be convinced that Jesus was alive within the sphere of God that he stood for. "He is risen," it was exclaimed.[33] Thus the one who stood with the marginalized and represented everyone who suffered from anything, from sickness to social injustice, was himself drawn up into a world of higher, transcendent meaning of God's absolute rule.

There can be no hedging of Pascal's bet. The idea that Christian hope rests on Jesus rising into the memory of his followers offers little more than a spectacular trivialization: in the end, it adds up to nothing. This belief makes much more sense as the consistent extension of faith in a God who loves what God creates. How could the world that elicits amazement and awe fall from the creating memory of the eternal Creator? On the contrary, to affirm that the memory of God is itself creative is to bank on the coherence and the morality of the universe. And not insignificantly, it contributes the conviction that my little part in the drama counts. To fully live in the moment is to hope for absolute meaning in the future. To reiterate a theme that echoes through ideas about the end of time: Eternal God spans temporality. Grasping the deep meaning of eschatology requires

---

33. Jesus's resurrection was not a wonderful external event that caused faith, but an object of faith and hope that gradually came to orient his disciples. The story of the disciples walking to Emmaus (Luke 24:13–35) and recognizing Jesus in the breaking of the bread is an allegory of the rise of Christian hope in resurrection. It completes the momentous consequence of the faith invested in Jesus and the salvation he mediated. For an extended examination of the epistemology and meaning of resurrection faith, see Roger Haight, *Jesus Symbol of God* (Maryknoll, NY: Orbis Books, 1999), 119–51.

the mystical insight into creation itself: it envelops everything with the Presence of God.

This chapter concludes the consideration of the three-part Ignatian interpretation of the gospel in response to the social sin of racism. That sin, extended over four centuries, carries potential scandal that is comparable to the Holocaust. The rule of God mediated by Jesus confronts a negative historical power with an alternative vision for a counter-historical power. This chapter outlines an Ignatian formula for internalizing a liberating Christian vision to make Jesus's message and the energy of God's rule an actual force in history. Each person, all Americans, formally or anonymously, are summoned by the Creator to participate in this historical project. The last two weeks of the Spiritual Exercises solidify the life-decision of the one making the Exercises by consideration of the crucifixion and resurrection of Jesus.

But there is more to be said. The following chapter doubles back on this social-theological interpretation of the gospel in response to racism in the United States. It concludes this interpretation of the Ignatian view of Christian spirituality by reflecting on its character as an all-embracing way of life.

VI
Union with God in Anti-Racist Action

The previous three chapters have analyzed the logic of an Ignatian view of gospel spirituality as a dynamic integration of three dimensions: recognition of sin, a turn to Jesus of Nazareth for inspiration in dealing with it, and a commitment in decision and action that responds to the situation by following the pattern of life found in Jesus's ministry. This chapter proposes a conclusion to this interpretation of the gospel by describing the Christian spirituality they help generate. Recall that the operative term "spirituality" refers to the way persons or groups lead their lives in the face of what they consider ultimate. While spirituality includes prayer, worship, and other religious devotions, these activities do not exclusively define nor are they a necessary component of spirituality as a comprehensive way of life.[1] But, at bottom, some ultimate source of trust, commitment, and

---

1. In other words, spirituality as a common human phenomenon is pluralistic and transcends religion.

hope organizes a person's life, centers a spirituality, and, like a heart, pumps its blood. This perspective shows that spirituality describes ordinary human behavior. The question, then, asks in broad terms what the Christian spirituality made explicit by the Spiritual Exercises looks like. The point of spirituality, its inner aim, lies in the bond between the life of a person or group and the ultimate reality that organizes their lives. This gives rise to the focused question of this chapter: How might one describe Christian spirituality shaped by the Spiritual Exercises in the face of racism?

The racist context of American social and cultural life both narrows the interpretation of Christian spirituality and opens its relevance to a more expansive range of meaning and consequence. Too often the secular and religiously plural spheres of public life force the language of spirituality into a private space. The sheer recognition of racism thus plays a crucial role here. Structural sin exists. It is an actual dimension of history. It refers to public patterns of unjust behavior that have become so internalized into society and culture that they may remain as invisible as the air one breathes, a part of normal or ordinary life. "This sin is both outside individual human freedom and within it, 'objective' and subjective at the same time. It inescapably qualifies all human behavior, every exercise of freedom."[2] Racism is a particular form of structural sin that has grown with the nation and become an endemic dimension of all facets of public life. It is found in education at all levels, in the systems of medical care, in business, law, government, and religious institutions. It reaches those who recognize it and those who

---

2. Roger Haight, "Sin and Grace," in *Systematic Theology: Roman Catholic Perspectives*, ed. F. S. Fiorenza and J. Galvin (Minneapolis: Fortress Press, 2011), 398–402 at 402.

do not. Racism exists and everyone participates in it. The question of this chapter thus becomes even more acute: How would we imagine union with God in the Ignatian form of Christian spirituality that responds to a racist context?

This chapter returns to the deep theological structure of revelation discussed in the first chapter: the object of revelation, the medium of revelation, and the interpretive reception and response to it.[3] That deep structure is reflected in the Exercises. The first dimension sets up a "theocentric" framework for understanding Christian spirituality. This is found in the bookends of the four weeks of the Spiritual Exercises. They begin with the Principle and Foundation and end with the Contemplation to Attain Love, both of which suggest a framework of creation theology and spirituality. Within the context of creation theology, after the consideration of sin that disrupts the basic relationship of creatures to the Creator, the second structural element of Christian spirituality is Jesus of Nazareth, interpreted as the Christ or the anointed one, who is the central revealer accepted by Christians as defining the relationship of human beings and all creatures to the Creator. The third element is found in the human response to God as revealed in Jesus's ministry. It expresses itself in a life-decision of commitment to God following the path of Jesus. Ignatius sums up this response in the two categories of contemplation and action bound together to form an integral human response. This integral response allows one to describe a union with God that in the American context includes anti-racist consciousness and ac-

---

3. This deep structure also reflects the three parts of the creed. God as Spirit correlates with God within human beings animating human response to mediated transcendent Presence.

tion. What follows represents this spirituality in terms of God's presence in creation, the mediation of Jesus, and a life inspired by God as Spirit.

Creation Spirituality

The Spiritual Exercises offer a program in Christian spirituality. Jesus of Nazareth stands at the heart of the Exercises; his ministry represents the rule of God for the full flourishing of what God creates and against everything that is injurious to human beings and God's world. Ignatius's Exercises reflect the structure of revelation outlined in Chapter I in which God as Creator is mediated by Jesus of Nazareth. Ignatius sets the contemplations on Jesus's ministry within a framework of creation theology. As just noted, the two exercises, one at the beginning and the other at the end of the program, appeal to a theology of creation: "Principle and Foundation" (SE, 23) and "Contemplation to Attain Love" (SE, 230–37). Highlighting the contribution of creation theology to the Exercises increases appreciation of the depth and expanse of the spirituality they mediate. The contribution of the paragraph Principle and Foundation is discussed here; the third part of the chapter will discuss the relevance of the Contemplation to Attain Love.

The paragraph entitled "Principle and Foundation" lays down two principles that should guide human life. The first is teleological: it states that human beings are created for salvation within the life of God. The second stipulates that all else in the created world is in service to human beings that they may achieve their end. The anthropocentrism of this second principle is widely questioned today. All created things have their own ontological value; by contrast, subordination to human destiny tends to support a mindset of domination that has led to serious planetary endangerment. But these principles can still serve as a foundation for a spiritual life without the anthropocentrism. While everything interacts in an interconnected world, means should not be confused with ends. A rule of life based on creation for salvation entails a judicious exchange with other creatures toward the goal of all existence and according to the nature of each entity.[4] This rule appears when Ignatius discusses a major decision about the use of life's resources (SE, 154). It bears continual relevance because a natural tendency leads people to subordinate the end to the means: to choose pragmatically on the basis of attraction and to resume consideration of their final goal thereafter. But, more importantly, it functions implicitly as a premise of the Exercises and a fundamental orientation of Christian spirituality because it tries to grasp the mystery of God's purpose in creating.[5]

It may be helpful here to appeal to the theology of creation to justify the critique of Ignatius's anthropocentrism and support the intrinsic value of other creatures that needs to be factored into Christian spirituality. Creation by God

---

4. This principle comes with creation theology, and John Calvin insisted on it in his theology of the spiritual life. Things should be used according to the end to which the Creator destined them. *Calvin: Institutes of the Christian Religion*, ed. John T. McNeill (Philadelphia: Westminster Press, 1960), III.x.2. Calvin's use of teleology is a good corrective of Ignatius's anthropocentrism.

5. George E. Ganss says of the Principle and Foundation that "it sketches the worldview of Christian faith as the background against which everything else in the Exercises and in life should be viewed." *The Spiritual Exercises of Saint Ignatius* (Chicago: Loyola Press, 1992), 148. It should not be forgotten that the Christian doctrine of creation subsumes into itself the personhood of God and that God creating is motivated by love of everything that God creates.

sets up a two-dimensional relationship between God and creature. The first relationship may be called dependence; all finite reality depends on the sustaining power of ongoing creation for its very existence. But at the same time, that very relationship establishes each creature's autonomous value, its unique value relative to other creatures. The creating power of God bestows on each creature an ontological value "in-itself" that protects it against abuse by other creatures. Thus, in its very foundations, the created world exists in a dynamic and fluid condition of moral ambiguity where, in evolutionary conflict, species prey on species for survival. This complicates the relation of human beings to other creatures. On the one hand, use of other creatures becomes a moral issue and requires deliberation and judgment. On the other hand, other creatures, especially other human beings in their individuality, gain a value in themselves because of their relationship with God that they would not have without it. Creation explicitly bestows personal and moral social dimensions on human spirituality in its relationship to the world. These are engaged at the most primal level of being human.

This speculative metaphysical worldview can make its way into conscious spiritual life; such was the intention of Ignatius. This can happen in two distinct ways. First of all, the principle may serve as an essential orientation of one's life. As such, it does not operate expressly in each choice, but provides a central motivational direction to one's life and an openness to the future. The formula expresses purpose, but purpose easily combines with a sense of time and can merge with an eschatological sense of ultimate destiny. This automatically bestows seriousness on existence and can also communicate a guiding orientation that expressly internalizes purpose and the temporal direction of one's life. It thus lifts the world as a sphere of operation above the merely pragmatic and at the same time establishes a basic attitude of all-embracing meaning and purpose.

A second dimension of the worldview may be called a reverence for being. A person with this fundamental moral reaction of reverence for reality "understands the dignity and nobility of being as such, the value which it already possesses in its opposition to mere nothingness."[6] The autonomy of each being means that it can never be reduced to merely a means without reflection and is always a subject of moral discernment.[7] This basic respect for the integrity of being itself loosely correlates with Ellacuría's first level of moral sensitivity to the autonomous weight of being itself alluded to earlier. The world itself is charged with moral responsibility for agents capable of recognizing it.

The metaphysical framework of Ignatius's Principle and Foundation helps to recast in a positive framework the deepest rationale for anti-racist commitment and activity. It widens the perspective for combating sin and sets it in a more constructive worldview. Without losing compassion, it enhances the need for militancy. Anti-racist activity not only entails beating back deep negative forces that plague history; it also proposes that human activity offers a constructive contribution to building more life-giving structures. As Juan Luis Segundo insisted, human freedom cannot be re-

---

6. Dietrich von Hildebrand, *Fundamental Moral Attitude*s (New York: Longmans, Green, 1950), 9. "Thus there is a value inherent in every stone, in a drop of water, in a blade of grass, precisely as being, as an entity which possesses its own being, which is such and not otherwise."

7. von Hildebrand, *Fundamental Moral Attitudes*, 10, echoing the categorical imperative of Immanuel Kant relative to human beings.

duced to the task of avoiding sin; it carries the power and opportunity to create new structures in society that actually enhance the value of human life that they so often repress.[8] The metaphysical grounding of the Exercises responds to the question of the source of the meaning of one's personal life, what it is dedicated to, where it is leading, and what it intends to contribute to and accomplish. The sin of omission relative to racism runs far more deeply than the idea that God is watching and keeping accounts. It is failure to seize an opportunity for participating more fully in a world of values and helping to make those values real by transforming them into action. When Ignatius's classical teleological statement of a worldview undergirding spirituality is transposed into a present-day picture of the universe and an evolutionary account of the world's emergence, it undergoes a metamorphosis into a metaphysics of co-creating in the power of God a world that reflects the rule of God.

Jesus as Mediator

The Principle and Foundation states Ignatius's worldview: a conception of created reality as heading purposefully and temporally toward eternal life with God. Jesus specifies the Christian spirituality contained in the larger context of creation theology. He "mediates" God to human existence. "Mediating" in this context means revealing and making present, neither without the other, the rule of God in his ministry. Under this subheading we address the role of Jesus of Nazareth as mediator of the rule of God, which builds

---

8. Juan Luis Segundo, "Ignatius Loyola: Trial or Project?" in *Signs of the Times: Theological Reflections*, ed. Alfred T. Hennelly (Maryknoll, NY: Orbis Books, 1993), 149–75.

into a foundational worldview of creation, an understanding of reality as temporally moving toward God. This consciousness, mediated by Jesus Christ, specifies faith and spirituality as Christian. What follows recapitulates this logic, applies it to racism, and prescribes an anti-racist program of life.

Jesus has consistently been called mediator across Christian tradition. Through his ministry he communicated content to a vague sense of God's presence and remains a constant inspiration for Christian life. Jesus so stimulated faith in God that people experienced salvation through his ministry and through the interpretive memory of it recorded in the New Testament. The idea of mediation indicates a function or operation, and the meaning of the salvation he communicated, rather than having a fixed single meaning in the New Testament, bears many different metaphorical expressions. It follows that the theological norm for understanding what Jesus mediated must be faithful not to a specific understanding of salvation but to the deep existential experience of being delivered (σωτήριος), freed, made whole, accepted, and authorized by God. This abstract description of salvation hides the many individual and communitarian ways that people encounter the salvation mediated by Jesus. "Salvation" opens up existential meaning that was encountered in Jesus's mediation and expressed in many different symbols that include the responsibility to live in a certain way.

Thinking of Jesus as mediator calls for some clarification of the relationships between God, Jesus, and what Jesus called the rule of God. That discussion cannot begin with a definition of God who must remain the nameless one; God remains the incomprehensible transcendent power that suffuses all of reality and is experienced as transcendent Presence that renders every imaginative portrayal anthropomorphic. The contrast of Creator and creature shows that Jesus was a human person who lived in Palestine during the first half of the first century.[9] The later theological interpretation of Jesus's person as combining two natures, human and divine, should not distract from recognizing that Jesus was a human being. The proper way of understanding a past historical event follows the path leading to the later interpretation, rather than projecting an interpretation from a later context back on the original phenomenon. One of the major contributions of Ignatius's Spiritual Exercises rests on representing Jesus, as best he could in the sixteenth century, as a human person acting in the flesh and addressing his Jewish community.

The meaning of the phrase "the rule of God" was discussed earlier as representing the intention of God the Creator for the world. Like "salvation," it has many variations, but the concept of "God's intention" opens up to the many different aspects and uses of the term: future/present, other worldly/this worldly, spiritual/material, individual/social, God's agency/human agents, aspirational/realistic. All of these dimensions can be found in Jesus's gospel-ministry so that association with the salvific will of God does not restrict its meaning but releases its capacious character.

The way God, Jesus, and the rule of God relate to each other may seem to be theologically esoteric, but it has bearing on basic Christian spirituality. Jesus preached the rule of God; gradually he came to be understood as also bearing it

---

9. Careful language is required to prevent the classical doctrine of incarnation from suggesting a preexistence of Jesus of Nazareth. The language surrounding the doctrine of incarnation almost entices the imagination in that direction and turns the doctrine of one person with two natures into fable.

in his own person. The New Testament presents Jesus as God's spokesperson and representative. And still later Jesus was understood theologically as being a person bearing two "natures" or kinds of being: human and divine. The basis of that doctrine, however, goes back to its grounding experience; in Jesus Christians recognize a salvific divine Presence. The relationship between the three terms (Christians, Jesus, and God) is both functional and ontological; its meaning resides in and depends on an experience of God's presence and rule within the ministry and person of Jesus and of God as Spirit at work in one's own life. The term "functional" does not mean fictional; it points to a real experience of a real dynamic Presence mediated by Jesus to other human beings. This does not make Jesus into a hybrid, a composite, a mixture that sets him apart from human beings. Rather he is a human person who bears and makes present something other than himself, the presence and rule of God.[10] What was actualized in him can be actualized in each person in an analogous way.[11]

What seems like a theological digression aims at opening up the narrative character of the rule of God and of Jesus's corresponding mediation. The metaphysical theological interpretation of the person of Jesus through the use of abstract

---

10. The best expression in a short space of the metaphysics of this dual agency in a single action is contained in Thomas Aquinas, *Summa Contra Gentiles*, Book III, chapter 70. It is not a christological passage, but the structure of the statement can be applied to christology. For an analysis of God present and acting in history, see Ignacio Silva, "Thomas Aquinas Holds Fast: Objections to Aquinas within Today's Debate on Divine Action," *The Heythrop Journal* 54, no. 4 (2013): 658–67.

11. It is important at this juncture to apply the christological maxim that the more one makes Jesus different from other human beings, the more one undermines the very point of incarnational language.

terms in statements such as "Jesus, as incarnate divinity, gives created 'nature' a new divine existence" has occasionally diverted attention from the way Jesus mediates God's salvation. By contrast, the gospels contain stories that bear witness to incidents that were handed down and portray Jesus mediating the rule of God. The saving events of the Jewish scriptures and the New Testament should be recognized as interpretations of events that were remembered, then shared in conversation, and then collected into written accounts of these memories: God working human salvation through agents. Liberation from Egypt and reception of God's law on Sinai were events, whether or not the accounts are empirical reports; the stories of early prophets and kings, and the release from Babylonian captivity tell of God's rule effected in history by agents. Psalms lament human sins, and Isaiah announces future hopes. Scripture refers to things that have happened or are promised. The rule of God does not refer to a static form of being. Its meaning transpires in life, which is essentially always in motion and creative. The rule of God does not apply to place, but everyone participates in it when their lives reflect the intentions of the Creator.

The idea that the rule of God remains an idea until it is turned into a concrete narrative, a conception that echoes Ellacuría's use of the term "historicization," helps to clarify how Jesus's behavior as teacher, prophet, and healer have a bearing on the spirituality of his followers. The roles that characterize Jesus's appearance or "persona" clarify his actions. He communicated an understanding of life according to God's will in parable, aphorism, and sermon. He saw with a critical eye those accepted behaviors that did not correspond with the spirit of Torah or the traditional ideals that mark Israel as a covenant people. The rule of God implies judgment in the sense of condemnation of actions that be-

tray God's rule; it includes criticism, censure, and denuncia-
tion. Jesus attended to those who needed healing, those
whose freedom was tied in knots by sickness or evil spirits,
and those marginalized by those with power in society. The
rule of God intends integrity of being and applies to physical, social, and spiritual well-being. Jesus taught and
demonstrated reverence for being; his prophetic judgment
shows ultimate respect for human beings rather than resentment or retribution. Reading Jesus's mediation in the narrative key in which it unfolded historically, rather than as a
sign of his status in being, helps to clarify how it affects
those who encounter the stories. The mediation occurs in
being caught up in the story and resonating with its dynamics rather than in recognizing an implicit claim to Jesus's personal authority. The possibility of being so moved is
available to everyone. Jesus did not mediate consciousness
of the existence or status of God to Jewish imagination, because these were a given and taken for granted. He mediated a pattern of life that corresponded with the intention of
the Creator, one that was in the tradition and that he actively
applied in a distinctive and timely way.

This narrative understanding of Jesus's mediation puts
anti-racism squarely within the sphere of the rule of God.
Anti-racist activity embodies the rule of God within the
world, and its existence contributes to the rule of God. Law
is a pale representation of the rule of God while it remains
aspirational; the law reflects but does not create nor by itself
constitute the rule of God. Abstract teaching may point to it
and parable may illustrate it. But the rule of God exists as
just relationships between people, when justice that is measured by the actual respect that human beings deserve from
other human beings is accorded them. Wherever unjust relationships exist, as they always will in this world, the rule

of God appears as a utopia that judges the situation and inspires commitment to overturn it. But the rule of God also exists; it is embodied and real; Christians regard Jesus as a demonstration of this. The rule of God materializes or becomes actual in history in this person and in those incidents or movements that correlate with Jesus's ministry. Whenever human beings act out the intention of the Creator, there is the rule of God. When people respect one another, and in that measure, the rule of God exists.

The fundamental dynamics of christology and Christianity appear in the ministry of Jesus. They are intrinsically Jewish, as was everything about him. The idea of mediation captures the this-worldly, historical, and active character of the way Jesus saves. When Jesus's person is situated and understood through his ministry, its impulse takes hold of his followers, and the content of his mediation and the relevance of his communication for human living fall into place. Christian spirituality fully appears as a following of Jesus. It is not that all anti-racist activity has to be Christian; it is rather that Christian spirituality is essentially anti-racist. Ignatius's final exercise, the Contemplation to Attain Love, throws more light on the dimensions of a Christian spirituality that embodies these directions.

Life in the Presence of God's Spirit

We turn to some themes and phrases that characterize Ignatian spirituality in order to show how they amplify the following of the Jesus of the gospels in a racist context. This chapter began with a consideration of creation theology because the evangelical message revealed in Jesus's ministry fits within a larger metaphysical framework of creation. With his consideration of the Principle and Foundation, Ignatius set the Exercises within a context of a world created by God. At the other end of the program of the Spiritual Exercises, the "Contemplation to Attain Love" also explores the implications of creation theology. The larger framework of creation does not compete with Christian revelation; it serves as a context for appropriating the initiative of God's love communicated in Jesus's ministry.

The "Contemplation to Attain Love" (SE, 230–37) refers to our loving response to God who first loves human beings as God's creatures. This dense contemplation contains three fundamental principles among others that contribute to the character of Ignatian spirituality. The first of these principles maintains that God is present and at work in all of creation.[12] Various aspects of God's immanent activity in the world make up the substance of the contemplation.

But the foundation rests on the stipulation that the effects of God creating cannot be distinguished from God's presence within the created world and its motivation. God is creating power and presence. This bears richer meaning today than in Ignatius's time because of the dynamic view of the universe that science represents to our imagination. Everything moves and evolves, from sub-atomic particles to an expanding universe, so that the creating and loving presence of God takes on the connotations of doing and acting as distinct from a kind of naked or vacant sustaining. God is the dynamic energy of being. The Contemplation to Attain Love presents various ways of parsing God's presence and activity in the world for human appreciation and response.

----

12. The theology of creation helps to clarify the reasons for the view of the immanence of God to all of reality as seen in the first part of this chapter. An understanding of the dynamics of creation helps to explain Ellacuría's category "theologal" referred to earlier in this work.

Ignatius highlights how, from various points of view, God's dynamic presence as Creator reflects a divine motivation of pure love. This supports the idea of finding God in all things because God acts in all things.

The second principle also supplies foundational support to an Ignatian interpretation of Christian spirituality. It states that "Love ought to manifest itself more by deeds than by words" (SE, 230). This typically practical side of Ignatius will be developed as an extension of the election or life-decision elicited within the context of the contemplations on the ministry of Jesus. Making decisions and acting them out form an essential dimension of gospel spirituality.

The third principle has the name or title of "contemplation in action." This phrase does not occur in the Contemplation to Attain Love but it may be considered as implied in it; the phrase was used by the contemporary trusted interpreter of Ignatius, Jerome Nadal.[13] It grows out of creation theology and God's immanence within the created order and functions as a way of drawing together the threads of the Spiritual Exercises into a distinctive and consistent Christian spirituality that can sustain meaning in life today. These three key phrases or ideas serve as an outline for this section.

Finding God in all things. The text of the Contemplation to Attain Love indicates that Ignatius wants the persons making the Exercises to *feel*, to experience in a personal existential way, that God is present to them in an active love. This should elicit a spontaneous response of love of God in return. A person should desire and ask for "interior knowledge of all

13. Joseph F. Conwell, *Contemplation in Action: A Study in Ignatian Prayer* (Spokane, WA: Gonzaga University Press, 1957), provides a short, careful examination in this principle based on early documents of the Society of Jesus.

the great good I have received, in order that, stirred to profound gratitude, I may become able to love and serve the Divine Majesty in all things" (SE, 233). The encounter with God's active love stirs a responding love for God. As God's love for us manifests itself in the dynamic action of creating, so too does human response express itself in action. Ignatius is not looking for a passing feeling or a "high." The metaphysical grounding of the meditation on creation, conjoined with Jesus's revelation of the rule of God, calls for a response in terms of a permanent disposition.

The Exercises outline such a response of reciprocal or responding love in four points. The first asks that a person call up into reflective consciousness all the gifts that God, in creating, has bestowed on each one. Those gifts define a person's individual identity; God has given to all their particular being. Each one's being is gift.[14] The proper response in Ignatius's view consists of a return dedication of one's liberty, memory, understanding, and will; only a complete return of one's personhood in love can begin to respond to the gift of God's loving creation of the self.

The next three points reinforce the intensely personal relation established in the first consideration. God dwells within all creation as a presence and thus God "dwells also in myself," continually gifting all persons with their inner selves. God labors and works "for me" by holding in existence not just me but also all things that surround and nurture me.[15] One should thus relate to God as to the source of

---

14. The evolutionary character of reality does not undermine the rationale of a theology of creation. It may however influence the language used to describe the emergent character of the created universe(s) and each person's identity.

15. This is probably the source for Pierre Teilhard de Chardin's metaphor of the second hand of God referred to in the preface.

all that is good in existence itself and its sustaining ground. These overlapping and intertwining considerations weave a world that is saturated with God's presence, one implicitly mystical in its scope. The contemplation is meant to suffuse the self with a consciousness of God's loving presence that is always there, creating, sustaining, working, appealing to each one for a loving response.

Is it possible to read Ignatius's interpretation of God's solicitation of a human return of love in a distinctive way when it is considered in the context of racism? Some basic commonsensical considerations can direct this aspect of Christian spirituality toward the actual socio-cultural world in which we live.

The metaphysical character of the Contemplation to Attain Love solicits a conscious deliberation on the structure of one's being as an intelligent, reflective creature, a real self who exists with agency. The grounding in creation theology lifts a person's relationship with God out of the context of an individual transaction and situates it in the context of being itself. It expands a person's selfhood; it places one in a world created by and belonging to God. It leads one into those fundamental moral attitudes spoken of earlier, the dispositions of gratitude and reverence for the world of which one is a part. It lifts one's most personal actions out of the idiosyncratic and places them in a common world along with others. It bestows on each one a personal responsibility for his or her life within a particular context that is part of a whole that is in turn subject to God's rule.

This profound context automatically bestows on antiracist instincts, perceptions, and basic reactions a sacral character. The reaction to God's love transcends the recognition of personal gifts to the self as individual and translates

God's active presence to the self into the context of a universal condition that includes a social imperative to seek the augmentation of all life. God's presence is always there; it is everywhere; people are always responding to God's presence, positively or negatively; the rule of God that Jesus preached reaches out expansively and fills all the spaces of human exchange. In this view of things, anti-racist reaction and behavior correspond with the rule of God that Jesus communicated. This does not describe a present-day external application, conceived apart from and laid on top of Jesus's message. It reflects the intrinsic logic of Jesus's teaching represented, for example, in the parable of the Good Samaritan as was shown earlier. Recall how Karl Rahner, reflecting the Johannine doctrine that the vehicle of loving God is the love of God's beloved, insisted that "one can love God whom one does not see only *by* loving one's visible brother lovingly."[16] The command to love your neighbor applies to everyone; it also manifests itself as a social categorical imperative emerging out of society itself.

Love shown in action more than words. Ignatius prefaces the Contemplation to Attain Love with an explicit statement of the cliché: "Love ought to manifest itself more by deeds than by words" (SE, 230). The maxim highlights the practical character of the New Testament: "You will know them by their fruits" (Mt 7:16). The rule opens up the can-do soldier-

---

16. Karl Rahner, "Reflections on the Unity of the Love of Neighbor and the Love of God," *Theological Investigations* (Baltimore: Helicon Press, 1974), 6:247. What modernity adds to this interpretation is an emphasis on the social dimension of this teaching. That social dimension is also present in Jesus's teaching within the scope of Israel and the whole Jewish community.

side of Ignatius and through him the inner logic of the gospels. The contemplations of Jesus's ministry lead up to a life-forming decision, and then they allow it to settle as they go on to consider how Jesus's own destiny unfolded. The decision that leads to action, a conviction or determination that guides one's life, makes Jesus and the rule of God he manifested the rudder of a person's voyage. It may be taken for granted that intelligence and understanding intrinsically orient people toward decision and action. But a short reflection on the bearing of this maxim on spirituality serves to reinforce the movement that the Exercises find in the gospel.

Coupling "decision" and "action" provides a distinct vantage point for considering the character of human life. Life extends over time; it forms a narrative, so that human life consists of a journey made up of a series of decisions and actions. The philosopher Maurice Blondel developed his philosophy around the notion of "action"; the category symbolizes human life itself in dynamic terms.[17] Blondel's notion of "action" roughly corresponds with the term "existence" but captures the intentional, voluntary, and dynamic character of human life. Action does not lie on the other side of knowing and willing as an attendant consequence. Life is action, and knowing and willing are themselves actions that serve the wider human range of doing, making, achieving, and living. One constructs oneself by one's action; action shapes, carries, and alters one's basic character. We are what we do, not in any exclusive sense that minimizes any constituent parts, but in a way that "doing" makes actual what one imagines, con-

---

17. Maurice Blondel, *Action (1893): Essay on a Critique of Life and a Science of Practice*, trans. Oliva Blanchette (Notre Dame, IN: University of Notre Dame Press, 1984), 434.

ceives, and plans. Action thus turns into a principle or a lens for measuring what is real when ideas come to the human person. This is consonant with what Ellacuría called historicization. The construction of the world and of the self are mixed up with each other. In both cases, the truth and viability of thought about the self and the world have to be tested by active engagement with what actually is.

The perspective on life as action that forms a narrative provides an angle from which to formulate what goes on in the doing or making of Ignatius's Spiritual Exercises. Ignatius constructed the Exercises as a sequential arranging of Jesus's ministry drawn from the gospel stories; he shaped them into an extended narrative. The person who does the Exercises as Ignatius conceived them follows a narrative of Jesus's ministry. In accordance with the basic formula for Christian spirituality as a "following of Jesus," the dynamics of making the Exercises can be understood as a "fusion of narratives." This means that persons who engage the program absorb the inner logic of Jesus's ministry as distinct from, but not separate from, the particularities of his time and place.[18] At the same time, they appropriate the inner dynamism of Jesus's life and, in the manner that is possible and appropriate, internalize it as their own. The point here consists of interpretation. Each one who makes the Exercises interprets their subject matter, but interpretation here unfolds on a level that should not be confused with narrow intellectual appreciation or parsing of concepts. It consists, rather, of a fusion of existential possibilities

---

18. The inner logic is also distinct from the particular chronology of the events. The point here is not the historicity of the details of gospel stories but the inner drive of the ministry.

drawn from the Jesus-stories for living one's own life into the future. This does not exclude intellectual acumen, but it reaches for what is going on when Ignatius uses the term "feeling" or sensing the path forward in one's own life.[19]

Before turning to the third principle for spirituality found in the Contemplation to Attain Love, which is contemplation in action, another insight from Blondel may be helpful. Blondel's philosophy of action gave him a distinct perspective on a theory of knowledge that saw the role that behavior, the practical doing of things, had in life-shaping knowledge. It is contained in what he called "possessive knowledge." Action mediates possessive knowledge, a knowledge that stands in contrast to abstract or conceptual knowing. Possessive knowledge stems from active engagement with something. Doing that engages a subject matter "contains the real presence of what, without it, knowledge can simply represent, but of what with it and through it is vivifying truth."[20] Blondel describes a kind of merger of beings here. Like a mechanic dealing with engines or a soldier with battle, one possesses what one knows because one is possessed by it. Engagement with reality outside the self brings it inside and makes it a part of the self. "The role of action, then, is to develop being [of the self] and to constitute it."[21]

---

19. As noted earlier, Ignatius's religious epistemology is complex, especially in dealing with discerning movements within the self. He favored "feeling" as a kind of primary contact with the reality of God's presence, prior to conceptualization and analysis but illuminated by them. Michael J. Buckley, "The Structure of the Rules for Discernment of Spirits," *The Way: Supplement* 20 (Autumn 1973): 19–37.

20. Blondel, *Action*, 434.

21. Blondel, *Action*, 425. Blondel also phrased these dynamics in this way: "The objective reality of beings is therefore tied to the action

This principle does not translate into this or that anti-racist action. Such considerations are contextual and unique to each individual. But it directly undermines deliberate ignorance: "I can't do anything about it." "I'm colorblind, and I never consider questions of race." These statements represent a positive disposition by their commitment to ignoring a situation that embraces the self whether or not one attends to it. Ignatius's cliché is matched by the human dilemma: in American racist society, not to be aware and not to act is a form of action.

Contemplation in action. The tension between prayer and action, where action takes on a more specific meaning of "doing things," has long been a theme in Christian spirituality. But the phrase "contemplation in action" has an Ignatian ring to it; it has its roots in God being present in all things as the Contemplation to Attain Love asserts. What follows is a way of understanding this phrase that does not consist in a historical exegesis of what Ignatius via Nadal meant by it, but a plausible interpretation for how one might understand and be inspired by the phrase in a busy twenty-first-century secular society and culture.

We begin by considering an integrated view of the relationship between contemplation and action. Both contemplation and the performance of a given task are actions: discrete forms of behavior. As such, they appear to have distinct goals that are different from each other. They compete with each other in terms of time spent and seem opposed in the respective introverted and extroverted character of each. Mental activity differs from physical

---

of a being who, in seeing, makes what he sees be, and who, in willing, becomes himself what he knows" (419).

work; physical stillness runs counter to active physical doing. Once distinguished, the question becomes one of putting them together into a reciprocal relationship. This can be done by alternating exercises of prayer and work, as some forms of monastic life arrange things. One can bind them together by making recent or future action the subject matter of contemplative prayer and by bringing transcendent thoughts to the workplace.

Another way of understanding the relation between contemplation and action regards them not as alternating activities, but as a single activity that is both contemplative and active at once. In this view, contemplation and action represent different levels of a single performing consciousness that are merged, not alternating. One way of explaining this coupling can use the idea of a fundamental moral attitude, as discussed earlier. A fundamental moral attitude is a form of consciousness that exists "below" or "beneath" immediate consciousness of this or that object.[22] A fundamental moral attitude is like a habit or a virtue, which in Thomistic epistemology consists of a characteristic of the human spirit and consciousness that leans a person toward this or that thought, motive, and action. Like a muscle, it may be weak or strong because built up by contemplative

---

22. As an example of a fundamental moral attitude, one might consider a commitment to a set of values that implicitly regulates behavior instinctively; the internalization spontaneously prohibits or urges a certain decision or action. The values are conscious because they are operative in conscious decision and action; but they may not be explicitly or reflectively conscious at any given time. George Ganss characterizes the perception and knowledge aimed at by the Exercises as cognitive in a way that "fills and satisfies the soul" (SE, 2) and "*becomes a habitual attitude of mind,* a frame of reference instinctively used to guide one's life" (Ganss's emphasis). *The Spiritual Exercises of Saint Ignatius,* 199n164.

exercises. It becomes a part of conscious decision and action in the complexity of human consciousness rather than lying alongside them.[23]

The theme of the relationship between contemplation and action has to be placed firmly within the framework of understanding the meaning of union with God. Spirituality consists in the way persons or groups live their lives in relation to the object of their faith. This relationship subsists across time; it forms the substratum of human life, a kind of bedrock that supports the various activities that occur in a lifetime and strengthen it in turn. The point of spirituality lies within this inner dynamic relationship that binds contemplation and action together. Contemplation is distinct from the actions that flow from it, and external actions motivated by contemplative convictions can strengthen the bond between them. The relationship with God should not be confused with a particular activity that occurs in a moment of time. The relation is something deep and ongoing, even though it remains subject to growth and change either through actions set aside and designated prayer or devotion or through ordinary life, whether guided by a faith tradition or not.

These distinctions, analyzed here in an abstract way, help to open up a view of how Ignatian logic can explain

---

23. Something analogous to this analysis is going on in Meister Eckhart's interpretation of the Mary and Martha story in Luke 10:38–42. He interprets Mary, the one who listened as Jesus spoke, as the contemplative, and Martha, who was distracted with serving them, as the active one. The text seems to put contemplation on a higher spiritual plane. But Eckhart sees Mary as still a learner, and depicts Martha as one who has integrated contemplation and action. She represents a person who is not less united with God at prayer or in serving others. The idea of action as a "reality principle" considered earlier gives Martha a certain edge here. Roger Haight, *Spiritual and Religious: Explorations for Seekers* (Maryknoll, NY: Orbis Books, 2016), 108–9.

how anti-racist behavior can constitute the basis of a Christian spirituality that unites one to God. That logic presupposes a faith in God, the creating power who sustains all being in loving presence to the world. This faith is mediated by Jesus of Nazareth, who represents for the Christian imagination the character of God and shapes God's presence to consciousness. The logic combines "finding God in all things," love expressed better in action than in words, and the integration of the object of contemplation into one's action. Ignatius lays before the imagination Jesus's ministry that reveals God's love for the world. In a situation marked by racism, the strongest possible reception and response to God's love takes the form of action that reflects the will and rule of God displayed in Jesus's ministry.

This analysis does not show that Christian faith has generated a higher form of anti-racism. History undoes that illusion. But it does show that racist ideology and behavior are anti-Christian. It also explains why, in a racist situation, anti-racist activity unites one to God and, as activity integrated with contemplation and a following of Jesus, constitutes the highest form of Christian spirituality.

Conclusion

This conclusion emerges from an extensive interpretation of Christian spirituality through the lens of the Spiritual Exercises. The argument shows three distinct levels of interpretation of Ignatius's Spiritual Exercises at work simultaneously. They relate to each other as distinct levels of appreciation or perspectives on the program of the Exercises. The first is theological, reflecting the structure of the discipline of Christian theology. The second level has been called the logic of the Exercises, the order of presentation that represents how Ignatius construed the problem of sin, the question of the elementary direction of a person's life, and an extensive constructive response to the ordering of one's life. The third level is still more practical and immediate and refers to the specific character of the sin that is being addressed.

A theological structure subsists in the Exercises whether or not Ignatius thought in those terms. It has three dimensions that in this work correspond to the structure of revelation: the object of faith that is mediated by revelation, the mediator of revelation, and the reception and interpretation of the revelation by those who receive it. The first dimension of this structure is reflected in the bookends of the Exercises: their initiating reflection, Principle and Foundation, and their closing contemplation, Contemplation to Attain Love, both of which draw on the theology of God as Creator. After the consideration of sin, the Exercises quickly turn to Jesus as the revealer of God, the one in whom Christian faith finds a representative of God's presence. The response to this mediation of God is a life that is christomorphic, that is, it takes on the form of following Jesus Christ in such a way that the spirituality becomes or gains the name Christian. The first chapter raises up this structure, which is conceived in modern theological terms in the face of today's world, in order to appropriate the language of the late medieval Ignatius into a present-day religiously pluralistic culture.

The second level of interpretation, called the logic of the Exercises, refers more immediately to the way Ignatius has set forth the Exercises. In three stages, he proposes the human problem of sin, turns to the ministry of Jesus of Nazareth as found in the gospels as a response to sin, and reaches an existential climax in a life-decision that shapes one's response to Jesus's revelation of God. These three stages are developed in the third, fourth, and fifth chapters of the book. When these stages are analyzed, they seem to reflect abstractly a chronological progression in the Spiritual Exercises. In actual life the stages are always organically interacting. They also resemble the logic of a negative experience of contrast. In the very recognition of the negativity of sin, one implicitly knows that things should be different, or becomes open to a revelation of what could be, and feels an impulse to actively resist the negativity. Internalizing the revelation mediated through Jesus results in the decision and action that undergird a Christian spirituality.

The third level of interpretation is still more practical because it focuses on a particular social and cultural sin that amounts in many cases to a scandal. Scandal in this case implies a situation that undermines the moral credibility of the institutions infected by it. In this case, attention is directed to the national sin of racism that also reaches into the churches and personal spiritual lives. The distinctive mark of this level of interpretation lies in its shift away from Ignatius's focus on personal sin to a consideration of social sin with its post-Marxian sensibility to the social determinants of human existence. This sin was described in the second chapter, but that depiction falls far short of the reality as it is experienced by those who suffer because of it. It may be impossible for one standing outside the direct experience of the effects of racism to depict it in words, and still more impossible to express its existential depth, breadth, and inescapability. Yet it has become part of American society and culture so that all participate in it—while not being its victims in the same way.

Following the logic of the gospels, recognition of this sin sends Christians to Jesus of Nazareth whose ministry, considered in relation to this sin, opens up a distinctively new perspective on Christian life in the face of this potential threat to their own faith. The churches that have remained predominantly white do not have a strong record in this matter. The climax of a life-decision in this context should be a way of life, a spirituality, that is attentive to, if not explicitly active in, reversing the tide and the effects of racism. In the measure that this application of the logic of the gospel and the Spiritual Exercises corresponds closely to the substance of Christian faith, it offers a constructive interpretation of what Christianity offers to life in America.

Acknowledgments

I am grateful for the support and inspiration of many in the writing of this book. The encouragement came in many forms over the period it took to do the research, plan the project, and write the manuscript. The whole project was nurtured by Union Theological Seminary where I taught for just short of twenty years. These matters are part of the fundamental ethos of the Union community.

I also received direct support from the local New York Theological Workgroup which has been meeting regularly for more than fifteen years. It is composed of Jeannine Hill Fletcher, Elena Procario Foley, Brad Hinze, Paul Lakeland, Michele Saracino, John Thiel, and myself. I submitted an article-length programmatic study of this project for our discussion and later collaborated in a dialogue with Jeannine on how to approach a discussion of concrete examples of racial discrimination. The group encourages critical integrity and is very supportive.

Thanks to Laurie Cassidy who knows critical race theory well and who gave me some good leads. LaReine-Marie Mosely also read the text and lent her expertise in Schillebeeckx and Black experience in support of the work.

Acknowledgments

Elizabeth Johnson supported this project since its inception and offered critique and encouragement along the way. Brian McDermott, SJ, a leading American expert on the Spiritual Exercises of Ignatius Loyola, read the manuscript and helped me bring some of my language back in line with Ignatius's text and intentions. He also encouraged the project of opening up the Exercises to the issue of racism.

Christopher Pramuk, a sensitive interpreter of the dynamics of race in the United States, read an earlier draft of the manuscript and offered finely calibrated suggestions for revision. His thorough understanding of the subject matter, appreciation of the tack, and incisive reading of an early version of the work greatly helped the final drafting of the theological argument.

Finally, I'm grateful to J. Matthew Ashley for his extensive and lucid work on the spirituality of Ignacio Ellacuría over the years. Although Ashley was not directly involved in this project, his work on Ellacuría provided insight into the pivotal analogy for using the Exercises to mediate the gospel into the social arena and the racial context of the United States.

Of course, the very message of this work is that the grace of mutual support abounds and is stronger than sin. And the natural response is gratitude.

Index

Index

and Jewish tradition, 100, 110,
143, 176, 178
as king, 102–3, 105
and lepers, 120, 124–25, 149
and love, 139–40
as mediator, 8–9, 14–15, 96–97,
101–2, 126, 138, 164, 168,
172–73, 175–77, 190
and ministry, xix, 8–10, 20, 22,
24, 95–98, 100–102, 105–8,
110, 131–33, 135–36, 155–58,
167–68, 178–80, 184–85
as product of Jewish community,
103, 107, 117, 142, 174, 177,
183n16
as prophet, 114–16, 118
and resurrection, 136, 162–64
and revelation, 6–9, 15, 98, 191–92
and rule of God, 105–6, 113, 127–
28, 138, 147, 149, 154, 164,
174, 183–84
and salvation, 123, 150–52, 176, 178
and sin, 95, 97–99, 129, 154, 165
as teacher, 109–11
Jesus: A Revolutionary Biography
(Crossan), 110n11
Jewish communities
during time of Jesus, 103, 107,
117, 142, 174, 177, 183n16
and Third Reich, 29, 43, 93, 109
Jewish tradition, and teachings of
Jesus, 100, 110, 143, 176, 178
Jim Crow laws, 27, 29, 38–39, 46,
55, 57, 84
Johannine doctrine, 118, 183
Jones, Absalom, 39
Jones, Camara Phyllis, 28n3

Kant, Immanuel, 131, 171n7
Kelly, Conor M., 86n21
Kendi, Ibram X., 51, 55n32
Kierkegaard, Søren, 7
King, Martin Luther Jr., 43, 60–61, 88
kingdom of God, xix, 105, 110

Lakeland, Paul, 19
Lasalle-Klein, Robert, 66n2
Latin American Bishops Confer-
ence, 65
Lazarus, 109–12
Levine, Amy-Jill, 142–44
liberation theology, 67, 75, 122,
159
Lincoln, Abraham, 38
Lord's Prayer, 106
love
and God, 181–84
and Jesus, 139–40
Lucifer, 127n27, 156. *See also* rule of
Satan
Luckmann, Thomas, 77–78
Luther, Martin, 7, 23, 139–40
lynchings, 41, 84–85

Marx, Karl, 77, 192
Massingale, Bryan, 53
McAuliffe, Patricia, 78–79
McGhee, Heather, 53–55, 58n39, 61
Meier, John, 121
Meister Eckhart, 189n23
Menakem, Resmaa, 59
Metz, Johann Baptist, 4, 79n16
Mills, Charles W., 137n11
Models of the Church (Dulles),
16n17
Mosely, LaReine-Marie, 78n15
Moses, Robert, 87n24

Nadal, Jerome, 180, 187
nationalism, 50
Nazism, 29, 44–45, 109
Newman, John Henry, 14
Niebuhr, H. Richard, 15n16, 90
Northrup, Solomon, 31, 37

oppression
and alienation, 159
and apocalyptic literature, 150
racial, ixn2